BUDDHISM

JOHN SNELLING was born in 1943 in Wales. After graduating in English and Philosophy and lecturing for a number of years, he travelled to the East, where his interest was awakened in Eastern religion and philosophy. He was general secretary of the Buddhist Society (1980–84) and was editor of the society's magazine, *The Middle Way,* between 1980 and 1987. His books include *The Sacred Mountain* (1983), *The Buddhist Handbook* (1987) and *Buddhism in Russia* (1992), as well as several books for children on Buddhism and mythology. He spent his last years living as a member of the Sharpham North Community based in Totnes, Devon. Members of this community share an interest in meditation and its application in daily life, giving talks, meditation sessions, retreats and workshops. John Snelling died in January 1992.

D1605875

New Perspectives

THE SERIES

New Perspectives provide attractive and accessible introductions to a comprehensive range of mind, body and spirit topics. Beautifully designed and illustrated, these practical books are written by experts in each subject.

Titles in the series include:

ASTROLOGY
by Janis Huntley

BUDDHISM
by John Snelling

CHAKRAS
by Naomi Ozaniec

COLOUR THERAPY
by Pauline Wills

CRYSTAL THERAPY
by Stephanie Harrison & Tim Harrison

HERBAL REMEDIES
by Vicki Pitman

I CHING
by Stephen Karcher

NUTRITIONAL THERAPY
by Jeannette Ewin

RUNES
by Bernard King

SHAMANISM
by Nevill Drury

TAI CHI
by Paul Crompton

YOGA
by Howard Kent

New Perspectives

BUDDHISM

An Introductory Guide to the Buddhist Tradition

JOHN SNELLING

ELEMENT

Shaftesbury, Dorset • Boston, Massachusetts
Melbourne, Victoria

© Element Books Limited 2000
Text © John Snelling 1990, 2000

First published as *The Elements of Buddhism* in 1990 by
Element Books Limited

This revised edition first published in Great Britain in 2000 by Element
Books Limited, Shaftesbury, Dorset SP7 8BP

Published in the USA in 2000 by
Element Books, Inc.
160 North Washington Street,
Boston, MA 02114

Published in Australia in 2000 by
Element Books and distributed by
Penguin Australia Limited,
487 Maroondah Highway, Ringwood,
Victoria 3134

Designed for Element Books Limited by
Design Revolution, Queens Park Villa,
30 West Drive, Brighton, East Sussex BN2 2GE

ELEMENT BOOKS LIMITED
Editorial Director: Sarah Sutton
Project Editor: Kelly Wakely
Commissioning Editor: Grace Cheetham
Production Director: Roger Lane

DESIGN REVOLUTION
Editorial Director: Ian Whitelaw
Art Director: Lindsey Johns
Project Editor: Nicola Hodgson
Editor: Julie Whitaker
Designer: Vanessa Good

Printed and bound in Great Britain by
Bemrose Security Printing, Derby

British Library Cataloguing in Publication
Data available

Library of Congress Cataloging in Publication
Data available

ISBN 1-86204-764-2

CONTENTS

Acknowledgements

I should like to thank the following for their kind help: Stephen Batchelor, Martine Batchelor, Ajahn Anando, Richard Hunn, Rob Preece, Roger Wheeler and Diana St Ruth.

'All the Buddha's teachings have just this single object –
to carry us beyond the stage of thought.'
Ch'an Master Huang-po

For my daughter Sarah Snelling with much love.

The publishers wish to thank the following for the use of pictures: AKG London Picture Library: 20, 51; The Ancient Art and Architecture Collection Ltd: 93; Art Directors and TRIP Photo Library: 104; British Museum Photographic Service: 38; Hutchison Library: 54, 85, 89, 97

INTRODUCTION

Many years ago, when I was trekking through the Nepalese Himalaya en route for Mount Everest, I found myself one evening in a small Sherpa village. With nothing better to do, I went over to look at the local Buddhist temple.

Inside all was dark, but gradually my eyes became accustomed to the gloom. Then I could see a phantasmagoria of benign and wrathful deities dancing on the walls, their once brilliant colours coated with brown soot from the butter-lamps that had flickeringly illuminated the temple for centuries.

My attention was drawn by the glint of gold and copper. I walked cautiously across the room, picking my way between vermilion pillars and among ancient moth-eaten cushions, to a small shrine. There I found a jumble of ancient votive objects. I began to examine them. Almost at once I was seized by a disquieting sense of being watched. I checked behind ... nothing ... to either side ... nothing ... When I looked up, however, a sharp pang of surprise went through me. A huge gilded Buddha was sitting, partially concealed, in a chimney-like shaft behind the main shrine, and he was staring down at me, a faint smile playing across those colossal lips, as though he was amused at my initial unawareness of his presence. It was so obviously a benign and good-humoured smile that I could only return it. It also seemed to be telling me something.

Though a slight enough incident in itself, it forged an important connection. I have been deeply involved in Buddhism ever since – delving into the great mystery of the Buddha's smile. This book is a brief summary of what I have discovered.

THE ORIGINS OF BUDDHISM

Buddhism is a jewel from the treasure-house of Indian spirituality. It emerged about 2,500 years ago in the central plain of the River Ganges, just south of the Himalayas. Over the centuries Buddhism has been transmitted to many other countries and in the process has absorbed much of local tradition and undergone exciting new phases of development, However, its Indian elements have always remained central and fundamental.

ABOVE BUDDHISM, WHICH IS BASED ON THE TEACHINGS OF SIDDHARTHA GAUTAMA, ORIGINATED IN INDIA SOME 2,500 YEARS AGO.

The established form of religion prevalent in India 2,500 years ago was Brahminism. Here a privileged caste of priests mediated between the ordinary people and the gods by controlling specialized religious rites. This tradition – the *Vedas* were its holy writings – was largely the creation of the dynamic Aryan people who invaded India during the first millennium BCE, though it also drew upon indigenous elements. Buddhism, on the other hand, emerged from an alternative and rather different religious stream, the origins of which predate the Aryan invasions. This is an ancient yogic tradition, originally without professional priesthood or formal organization, which places primary emphasis on direct personal penetration of the ultimate mysteries of life.

Since time immemorial pious Indians have venerated those spiritual seekers who have gone off alone into the tangled mountains and untamed jungles to discover truth for themselves. A sophisticated spiritual technology evolved to meet their needs: special yogas and meditation practices that, if correctly and diligently applied, might open the eye of wisdom and reveal Ultimate Reality, which is always sought within – in the human heart.

Although originally unsystematic and anarchic, around 600 BCE some groups of yogis, who had gathered around particular teachers or shramana, began to feel the need to present a more coherent and organized face to the world. New prosperity had created bustling commercial towns and cities populated by classes of nouveaux riches who had both the leisure and inclination for philosophical and religious inquiry. The Buddha was just such a teacher, and it was from among the 'young men of good family' that he drew many of his first disciples.

THE WHEEL OF LIFE

In order to understand Buddhism, it is useful to have a clear idea of the cosmology in which its teachings evolved.

Fundamental is the idea that time is not linear but circular. Consequently, the Universe is not created out of nothing at a particular point, nor will it be completely destroyed at another; it has always existed and will always exist. In the meantime, however, it goes

ABOVE A TIBETAN TANKA (RELIGIOUS PAINTING) REPRESENTING THE BUDDHIST WHEEL OF LIFE. IT DEPICTS THE SIX REALMS OF EXISTENCE.

through endless cycles of creation and destruction, creation and destruction – over and over and over ...

Any being that is born into this cyclic Universe is the result of something that has gone before; or, in Buddhist parlance, he, she or it is the fruit (vipaka) of a preceding cause or willed action (karma). This is the doctrine of creation by causes. In turn, when any being dies, he, she or it creates the causes for the birth of a new being. All of us, then, are not living separate, individual lives, but are links in an endless circular or spiralling chain that reaches back into the beginningless past and forward into the endless future. This is not precisely reincarnation, for it is not exactly the same being that commutes from body to body down through the procession of the ages. The vital connection between one life and its successor is more subtle than that. We can say that it is not the same being that moves along the chain, but not a different being either; or we can say it is both the same and a different being. The appropriate word to describe this process is 'rebirth'.

REBIRTH

Classical Buddhism specifies five or six realms or 'destinations' in which it is possible for rebirth to take place (*see* box p.11). Now, the main problem bearing on any human being is that their next rebirth may not be in the human realm. In fact the odds are very heavily loaded against it. Only two destinations are pleasant; the rest are painful, most direly so.

What keeps Samsara, the wheel of cyclic existence, in perpetual spin? Basically it is trishna – thirst/craving/desire – not merely in its gross forms of wanting desirables and not wanting undesirables, but in extremely subtle ones, such as the basic undercurrent wish to exist. Trishna arises on a basis of delusion/ignorance (avidya), which is not just a blissful not-knowing but a kind of wilful blindness that refuses to face the true reality of a Universe of constant change and suffering. Anger/hatred, dvesha, joins trishna and avidya to form an unholy Gang of Three, often called the Three Fires or Poisons.

This points directly to the main objective of Buddhism. This is not, as in the Western religions, to worship a Creator God. Nor is the highest aim of Buddhism to ensure access to some kind of eternal heaven after death. No, what the Buddha sought was an Exit – final and total release from cyclic existence; escape from *Samsara* once and for all; never again to be subject to rebirth and its attendant miseries. This is Liberation, Moksha, Enlightenment, Nirvana ...

THE REALMS OF REBIRTH

1 the heavens (the realms of the devas or gods,
   plus some rarefied regions above them)
2 the realm of the asuras or titans
3 the realm of humans
4 the realm of animals
5 the realm of preta or hungry ghosts
6 the hell realms

11

LIFE OF THE BUDDHA

The historical Buddha remains a shadowy figure, though time has enlarged his life story and embellished it with a complexity of miraculous and marvellous detail. He was apparently born around 566 BCE into a leading family of one of the small tribal republics that had sprung up in northern India. The domains of his people, the Shakyas, were situated right beneath the Himalayan foothills, part of them in what today would fall within the Nepalese Terai. Consequently he is sometimes called Shakyamuni, the 'Sage of the Shakyas'; his personal name was Siddhartha Gautama.

THE EARLY YEARS

Legend has it that soon after Siddhartha Gautama was born it was predicted that he would either become a great world leader or a great religious teacher. His father, Shuddhodana, was determined that this should not happen, and took steps to prevent the boy from seeing anything that would turn young Siddhartha's mind towards religion, particularly signs of suffering in the world. So, Siddhartha spent his childhood and youth in luxury, and consequently, grew up knowing little of the realities of life. He married his cousin, Yashodhara, who in due course gave birth to a son, Rahula. However, despite his father's efforts, Siddhartha saw

ABOVE SIDDHARTHA GAUTAMA, THE HISTORICAL BUDDHA, RENOUNCED HIS LIFE OF LUXURY FOR THE QUEST FOR ENLIGHTENMENT.

12

ABOVE THIS TEMPLE CARVING FROM JAVA DEPICTS A SCENE FROM THE EARLY LIFE OF THE BUDDHA.

four signs that changed his life. Firstly, he saw three signs of the presence of suffering in the world – a decrepit old man, a sick man and a corpse. He then met a sadhu or holy man. The sadhu possessed an air of calmness and a nobility of bearing that suggested to Siddhartha that he had come to terms with old age, sickness and death.

Siddhartha left his life of wealth and privilege. He exchanged his fine silk robes for the ragged ones of a holy man and wandered off into the world, alone and unsupported, to find an answer to the problem of suffering. He was about 29 years old.

THE NOBLE QUEST

Siddhartha spent the next six years on an intensive spiritual quest. He studied meditation at jungle retreats from the foremost yogic teachers of his day. He also experimented with extreme ascetic practices: living in graveyards, sleeping on beds of thorns, frying in the noonday heat and freezing beneath the moon at night. He starved and punished his body in the hope that he could root out all desire. Again he applied himself so wholeheartedly that he attracted an admiring circle of five fellow yogis. He also brought himself to the verge of death. Then, at the eleventh hour, terminally weak and emaciated, he realized that he had still not found what he was looking for and would probably die if he persisted. So he abandoned his austerities and took a little food, a lapse that so disgusted the five yogis that they declared, 'Siddhartha has taken to the easy life!' – and promptly abandoned him.

13

ENLIGHTENMENT

One day Siddhartha sat beneath a bo tree – at a place called Bodhgaya, which lies in the modern Indian state of Bihar – and vowed that he would not leave that 'immovable spot' until he found an answer to the riddle of suffering.

On the 49th day, Siddhartha's mind became as calm and bright as a mirror, so that he was able to have clear insight into the basic mechanisms that create and sustain samsara. He relived his own innumerable past births in the different ages of the world. Then, turning his attention to others, he saw how they circulated through the cycles of birth and death, and that the way in which they passed on was determined by the moral quality of their actions (karma). He then considered how the 'defilements' (sensual desire, ignorance and so on) that cause suffering could be extirpated and, seeing that it was indeed possible to do so, he was himself freed. He lastly surveyed the 12 links of the chain of Dependent Origination, which in effect describe how birth inevitably leads, by way of a series of predictable stages, to death, which is a prelude to yet another birth – and one that will merely turn the Wheel of Life through another repetitious revolution unless the process is stopped. Siddhartha was now the Buddha: the 'One Who is Awake', the 'One Who Knows'.

THE TEACHING CAREER

So began a 45-year ministry (531–486 BCE) during which the Buddha wandered between the towns, villages and cities of the middle Ganges plain, mainly in the ancient kingdoms of Magadha and Kosala, spreading his teachings.

Though many of his early followers were lay-people, there were also those who wished to give up the world and family life in order to devote their time and energy entirely to the Dharma. So emerged the Sangha, the community of Buddhist monks, to which later nuns were admitted. At first the Sangha lived lives of extreme simplicity as homeless mendicants, dressing in rags, living only on alms-food and seeking shelter in caves and beneath the roots of trees. Later, however, thanks to the largesse of wealthy lay benefactors – the Buddha numbered among his devotees kings, aristocrats and rich merchants – they obtained more permanent and comfortable residences during the Monsoon Season. These were the beginnings of vihare: Buddhist monasteries.

PASSING INTO PARINIRVANA

The Buddha died around 486 BCE, when he was about 80 years old. His disciples, both monastics and laity, gathered around where he finally lay in a grove of sala trees in Kushinagara, not far from his birth-place at Lumbini. His last words to them were a pithy encapsulation of his whole teaching:

'Impermanent are all created things. Strive on with awareness ...'

Then he passed into Parinirvana, an ineffable state utterly beyond the scope of ordinary mental comprehension or verbal description.

15

ABOVE THIS MAP SHOWS THE MAIN AREAS OF BUDDHIST INFLUENCE IN THE INDIAN SUB-CONTINENT.

THE DEVELOPMENT
OF BUDDHISM

CHAPTER TWO

Although Buddhism has not been a significant religious presence in India for many hundreds of years, it did thrive in the subcontinent for over 1,000 years after the death of the Buddha. During that period it underwent many important developments. We can trace the emergence of three major traditions or new 'turnings of the wheel of the Dharma', each with its own component schools and sects.

BASIC BUDDHISM

Though, by virtue of his attainment, he possessed a certain natural authority, the Buddha never tried to set himself up as a leader figure, nor did he nominate a successor. He just indicated that, if there was a need for guidance after his death, his followers might look to his Dharma, his teachings.

Soon after his death, however, the Buddha's monks and nuns came together from far-flung regions and held a great council, the first of several, at which the teachings were orally rehearsed. An 'authorized version' was eventually agreed upon. It was then committed to memory by specialists and transmitted by word of mouth for more than 400 years. A written version was not produced until the first century CE in Sri Lanka. This huge body of scriptures is called the *Pali Canon* after its medium, Pali, one of the ancient dead languages of India. An alternative name is *Tripitaka* or 'Three Baskets', on account of its division into three main sections:

THE THREE BASKETS

1   The Vinaya Pitaka or Basket of Discipline, which includes the code of rules by which monks and nuns should live.

2   The Sutra Pitaka or Basket of Teachings: the collections of instructional discourses of the Buddha.

3   The Abhidharma Pitaka or Basket of Higher Teachings. The compilers of Abhidharma extracted and systematized the basic philosophical ideas implicit in the Buddha's teachings.

17

During the 400-year oral phase of Buddhism many small changes crept in. So, while it might be tempting to regard parts of the *Pali Canon* as Buddhavacana, the Word of the Buddha, it would perhaps be a little unwise, as well as contrary to the non-fundamentalist spirit of Buddhism to do so. The wisest course would rather be to read and study the scriptures with an open mind, one that is both appreciative and critical, with a view, not so much to fixing a literal understanding in one's mind, but of assimilating the underlying spirit.

MAHAYANA BUDDHISM

The Buddha himself foresaw that his teachings would, by stages, lose their vitality and effectiveness. However, by skilfully leaving things flexible and open-ended, the Buddha allowed for new waves of creativity and development to periodically revitalize the tradition that he had set going. The first of these was the Mahayana, the so-called 'Great, Vehicle'.

What is the Mahayana? The word is really a kind of portmanteau term embracing a whole range of different developments that began to arise among the Buddhist faithful a few hundred years after the Buddha's death. These are definitely *Buddhist*; that is, their proponents primarily revered the Buddha and adhered to his basic teachings as well as the goal of Enlightenment. But they also represented the blossoming of hidden potentials that had hitherto lain latent within the tradition. They may have been initiated in one place, but they may equally well have arisen synchronously in different locations at more or less the same time.

Over centuries these developments began to be associated with a definite movement whose members consciously thought of themselves as Mahayanists as opposed to their precursors, whom they rather disparagingly dubbed 'Hinayanists'. However, as good and tolerant Buddhists, the followers of both traditions must by and large have understood that they were united in something larger than their differences. We know from the reports of travellers, for instance, that, even as late as the eighth century CE, both Mahayanists and Hinayanists were living side by side in the same monasteries in India.

Doctrinally, Mahayanists replace the spiritual ideal of the arhat, the 'noble one' who is assured of Enlightenment, with that of the bodhisattva. The orthodox Mahayana view is that the arhat has attained the salvation of nirvana for his own benefit alone, and has therefore achieved a lesser and, it is hinted, rather selfish goal. By contrast, the bodhisattva is motivated altruistically. He seeks nirvana, not for himself, but in order to help others. In this respect he is very much like a buddha – and indeed within the Mahayana the concepts of buddha and bodhisattva seem to blur into each other.

THE THREE BODIES OF THE BUDDHA

In the Mahayana, the Buddha is seen as the manifestation of a supramundane principle rather than as a flesh-and-blood person. In order to appear as he has in many different realms and times, 'he' has three wonderful bodies at his disposal:

1 The Nirmanakaya, the body in which he appears in the world (though this is not a 'real' body but a magical conjuration for compassionate purposes).

2 The Sambhogakaya, in which he appears in celestial realms to teach bodhisattvas and their ilk.

3 The Dharmakaya, a kind of cosmic body cognate with the Absolute Dharma, the quintessence of Buddha-qualities, the consummation of Shunyata, or emptiness, (see p.40).

The historical Buddha is also now often called Tathagata: he who has realized 'thus-ness' or 'suchness' (tathata).

Pre-Mahayana Buddhism was very much focused in the monasteries and concerned with the heroic struggle for nirvana by personal effort alone. It was therefore not for the ordinary man but for the educated elite and the dedicated few prepared to renounce the world. Lay people inevitably began to demand a more substantial spiritual status and these new forms were therefore evolved so that they could express simple faith and also, aware of their own limitations, call for help from outside agencies.

At the other end of the spectrum, for the spiritually sophisticated, new trends and schools of philosophy emerged, all of them highly esoteric. These again undoubtedly emerged to meet real needs. Many of the pre-Mahayana schools of philosophy were losing their edge and beginning to deviate, if only slightly, into the swamps and mires of false views. The new wave of Mahayana philosophers therefore set about devising new philosophical methods and systems that would lead to right views: that is, views consistent with what the Buddha had actually taught. So these were, in a sense, not so much new philosophies as newly-devised upaya or 'skilful means' for arriving at direct perception of old truths.

VAJRAYANA OR TANTRIC BUDDHISM

The traveller in India today can still, in certain religious centres, come across that disturbing kind of sadhu or holy man in whom those perennial irreconcilables, asceticism and eroticism, are brought together. He goes about naked, his body smeared with ashes, his beard and hair long and matted, coloured hieroglyphs daubed on his forehead, and a wild, even crazy look in his eyes. This is a tantrika, an adept of Tantra, it is whispered; he frequents charnel grounds and other macabre places, performing unspeakable rites and practices.

Such holy men are spiritual anarchists. They turn the prudent conventions of orthodox religion on their head. Yet, in tolerant India, it has never been denied that their Tantric path is a valid one, even though it may not be suitable for all seekers.

LEFT VAJRASATTVA, THE PRIMEVAL BUDDHA OF TANTRIC BUDDHISM, HOLDS A THUNDERBOLT (VAJRA), SYMBOLIZING ETERNITY, AND A BELL, FOR THE WORLD IS TRANSIENT LIKE THE SOUND OF A BELL.

We do not know much about the origins of Vajrayana Buddhism, but by the seventh century CE it had become well established. Vajrayana, comes from the term vajra, being a Buddhist symbol derived from the mythical thunderbolt of the Indian god Indra: a massive discharge of protean energy that blasts away delusion and inaugurates Enlightenment. It is a very appropriate symbol, for the Tantric path is claimed by its devotees to be a very speedy one, accomplishing in just one lifetime what might take countless lifetimes in the Hinayana or Mahayana.

The aim of Tantric practice is to transform one's body, speech and mind into those of a fully-enlightened buddha by special yogic means. To this end a variety of ritual and magical methods have been devised, involving the use of specialized forms such as mandala (*see* p.67), mantra (sacred formulae) and mudra (hand movements), and objects such as the vajra, the ritual dagger (phurba), the bell (ghanta) and the hand-drum (damaru). The power of such things lies in the fact that, in Tantra, everything is invested with cosmic energy. A simple sound may therefore, by virtue of its inherent quantum charge, produce powerful spiritual effects. Tantric practitioners also work with special deities (known in Tibetan as yidam), which may be benign or wrathful but are always imbued with enlightened qualities.

21

Tantra has its own sacred texts – a 'tantra' is a scripture – but it places primary importance on the guru. He is the guide who can steer the student through the perilous phantasmagoria of the psycho-spiritual world to the safe shore of Enlightenment. In the eyes of the student, the guru should appear equal to the Buddha. Tantra is also veiled in secrecy – this has contributed to much confusion about it, and practice cannot begin without the rite of initiation (abhisheka),

ABOVE THE BELL (GHANTA) IS USED IN TANTRIC RITUALS. ITS SOUND IS BELIEVED TO PRODUCE POWERFUL SPIRITUAL EFFECTS.

when the initiate steps into the mandala of his chosen deity. Even today one can hear exponents of reformed Vajrayana declare that their system leads more quickly to a higher realisation than is available in the other traditions. And yet the very thing that gave the Vajrayana its regenerative power – that is, its anarchic quality – has to a large extent been reformed away in the interests of creating a kind of 'safe' Tantra.

THE DECLINE OF INDIAN BUDDHISM

Buddhism gradually went into decline in India after about the seventh century CE. By the 13th century it was to all intents and purposes a dead letter. Popular mythology has it that it was the Muslim invasions that destroyed it, or the degenerate influence of Tantra. Yet there were other more significant factors, not least that the ongoing Hindu tradition, with its greater flexibility and involvement with the ordinary life of the people, gained new vitality and reabsorbed much of Buddhism into its own mainstream. Buddhism suffered from being concentrated in the monasteries too, some of which, such as Nalanda and Vikramalashila, had grown into great monastic universities where a whole range of spiritual arts and sciences were taught. When the Muslims did attack, the already weakened Buddhists were easily located, and 'liquidated'.

THE SPREAD OF BUDDHISM

The decline and fall of Buddhism in India was not the end of the story by any means. Buddhist teachings and practices had already been transmitted far beyond the confines to the sub-continent to places where, coming in contact with new influences and circumstances, they were in time to undergo further revitalizing phases of development.

WHERE DID BUDDHISM SPREAD?

The spread of Buddhism can be divided into three main areas of movement:

1 A Southern Transmission that took Buddhism down into many south-east Asian areas that fall within the boundaries of the contemporary states of Sri Lanka, Burma, Thailand, Laos, Kampuchea.

2 A Northern Transmission, that took Buddhism up into north and east Asia: into Tibet, China, Mongolia, Korea, Japan, Vietnam and so on.

3 A Modern Western Transmission, that in the past 100 years has brought Buddhism to Europe and North America – and to other parts of the world as well.

ABOVE OVER THE CENTURIES BUDDHIST PHILOSOPHY AND PRACTICE HAS SPREAD TO NORTH, EAST AND SOUTH-EAST ASIA. MORE RECENTLY, IT HAS BECOME POPULAR IN THE WEST.

BUDDHISM AND WISDOM

Buddhist teaching and practice is traditionally broken down into three categories: firstly shila, or moral restraint, secondly, samadhi, 'concentration', meditation and lastly prajna, wisdom.

All three should be developed more or less simultaneously, for when one advances at the expense of the others there will be imbalance. If, for instance, wisdom is undeveloped or lacking, it may be impossible to understand the insights that arise in meditation. On the other hand, without meditation, any understanding gained will be just ideas in the mind and hence not fully realized. Finally, without morality one may not have the necessary containing power to handle the very powerful psycho-spiritual energies that may be freed during meditation practice.

We will look at wisdom in this chapter. Wisdom is, in a sense, both the beginning of the path and the end, where it assumes an altogether higher or transcendent form. The wisdom that lies at the beginning is a grasp of the Buddha's basic teachings. These are not rigid articles of faith that we have to embrace totally. The Buddha recognized that truth cannot be pinned down once and for all. What held good last week or year is superseded in the changed conditions of today. 'Can you nail down the clouds in the sky, or tie them up with rope?' asks the Zen master. So, the Buddha's teachings should be regarded as skilful means (upaya) for obtaining certain results. We are invited to experiment with them to see if they work for us, in the context of our own everyday lives.

DUHKHA

It was the problem of duhkha, rather than abstract questions such as 'Who made the world?' and 'What happens to us after death?', that shocked the Buddha into his own spiritual quest.

The word duhkha is often translated as 'suffering' but, in fact, it covers a whole spectrum of psycho-emotional states, from a mild sense that things are not quite right to intense physical and mental pain. It may also be taken to mean that there is no lasting peace or rest in life; that we are forever under pressure and subject to disruption. This should not be taken to mean, however, that Buddhists believe that life is all suffering – a common misconception. The opposite of duhkha, sukha – pleasant feeling – is fully admitted. But pleasure and its ancillaries present us with few problems. Duhkha is problematic, however, and that is why we need to do something about it.

Of course, the human race is endlessly optimistic. It can devise new possibilities for hope, even in the direst circumstances; it can also invent ingenious ways of blanking out the dark or painful side of life. In our own age, with its wall-to-wall entertainment, we have become particularly adept at this. All of which might be applauded as a sign of good spirit if it did not contain an element of wilful blindness – a refusal to see things as they really are – the dark side as well as the light.

The person that desires to have *only* pleasure and refuses pain expends an enormous amount of energy resisting life – and at the same time misses out enormously. He or she is on a self-defeating mission in any case, for just as we evade certain forms of suffering we inevitably fall victim to others. Underlying our glitzy modern consumer culture there is a deep spiritual undernourishment and malaise that manifests all kinds of symptoms – nervous disorders, loneliness, alienation, purposelessness.

25

So blanking out, running away or burying our heads in sand or videotape will take us nowhere in the long run. If we really want to solve our problems – and the world's problems, for they stem from the same roots – we must open up and accept the reality of suffering with full awareness, as it strikes us, physically, emotionally, mentally, spiritually, in the here and now. Then, strange as it may seem, we will reap vast rewards. For suffering has its positive side – from suffering we derive the experience of depth, of the fullness of our humanity. This puts us fully in touch with other people and the rest of the Universe. Suffering can also bring out the full grandeur of our race, its heroic and best potential.

The great US writer Henry Miller wrote:

'Only in sorrow and suffering does man draw close to his fellow man; only then, it seems does his life become beautiful.'

If, therefore, we want to live as wholly human beings, we must be prepared to follow the old heroes willingly and consciously into the dark labyrinths and confront the grim denizens that lurk there. All we have to fear is our fear. All we need for protection is courage – and a little wise guidance.

SKANDAS

If the idea of 'I' is a fiction, we may justifiably ask how it arises in the first place. The classic Buddhist answer would run along these lines:

If we take a motor car, for instance, we feel quite sure about what we have, until we start taking it apart. But once we have removed the bodywork, stripped down the engine, taken out the gearbox and transmission, removed the wheels and so on – what's left? We don't have a car any more, just a set of spare parts.

It is the same with a person. That too can be stripped down to its basic components, which are traditionally divided into five standard categories: the so-called skandhas or 'groups'.

DELUSION AND 'NOT-SELF'

A primary cause of suffering is delusion: our inability, because of a subtly wilful blindness, to see things the way they truly are but instead in a distorted way. The world is in fact a seamless and dynamic unity: a single living organism that is constantly undergoing change. Our minds, however, chop it up into separate, static bits and pieces, which we then try mentally and physically to manipulate.

One of the mind's most dear creations is the idea of the person – and, closest to home, of a very special person, which we call 'I': a separate, enduring ego or self. In a moment, then, the seamless universe is cut in two. There is 'I' – and there is all the rest.

That means conflict – and pain – for 'I' cannot control that fathomless vastness against which it is set. It will try, of course, as a flea might pit itself against an elephant, but it is a vain enterprise.

Central to the Buddha's teaching is the doctrine of anatman: 'not-self'. This does not deny that the notion of an 'I' works in the everyday world. In fact, we need a solid, stable ego to function in society. However, 'I' is not real in an ultimate sense. It is a 'name': a fictional construct that bears no correspondence to what is really the case. Because of this disjunction all kinds of problems ensue.

Once our minds have constructed the notion of 'I', it becomes our central reference point. We attach to it and identify with it totally. We attempt to advance what appear to be its interests, to defend it against real or apparent threats and menaces. And we look for ego-affirmation at every turn: confirmation that we exist and are valued. This is, however, a narrow and constricted way of being. Though we cannot see it when caught in the convolutions of ego, there is something in us that is larger and deeper: a wholly other way of being.

THE FIVE SKANDAS

1 the category of the physical, which includes the body and its five senses
2 that of feeling
3 perception
4 mental formations (impulses and emotions)
5 consciousness or mind

When these groups of components come together in proper working order, the right conditions exist for the illusion of a self and a person to arise. But once they break down and go their separate ways – as at physical death, for instance – then that self or person cannot be found. What remains is not nothingness, annihilation, however. The Buddha defined that as a wrong view. Nor is it some sort of eternal something – another wrong view. There is an elusive 'middle way' transcending both annihilationism and eternalism – in fact all dualities, including life and death. We must seek the truth here.

DHARMAS

In the Abhidharma, the philosophical systematisations of the early Buddhist schools, the search for the ultimate elements of the world-process is taken as far as it will go on the micro level. These ultimate elements are called 'dharmas' – in the Sarvastivadin system there are 75 in all – and are said to be insubstantial appearances. Perpetually in a state of agitation –- rather like minuscule Mexican jumping beans, perhaps – until finally calmed in nirvana, they are forces rather than substances.

True reality, then, is the dance of these mysterious, evanescent dharmas as they cluster into groups and flow in what appear to be streams (santana). The deluded mind, however, discerns 'things' and 'personalities' here, just as a person looking up into the sky may see the shapes of faces or maps or trees where in fact there are just configurations of cloud; or a thirsty person in a desert may see a lake of cool water that is in fact only a mirage.

The teaching on dharmas – as indeed all the other of the Buddha's teachings – is not meant to be accepted on trust. The dedicated practitioner should actually be able to make his mind so calm, clear and still that he can actually see these infinitesimal 'flashings', of which there are many, to the split second. In this way he will once and for all see through the shadow play world of conventional existence and never again be its dupe. Needless to say, of course, only a very gifted meditator practising in ideal circumstances for many years will be able to reach this kind of virtuoso level.

DEPENDENT ORIGINATION

A popular explanation of the way causation works in the cycles of life and death is set out in the teaching of Dependent Origination (Pratitya Samutpada). We have already seen how the Buddha rejected the notion of a Creator God or Prime Mover. All phenomena in the Universe are produced within the cosmos by internal causes. That is to say, each phenomenon is the cause of a further phenomenon, which in its turn will go on to be a cause of something else, and so on, ad infinitum.

This sounds difficult, but we have similar ideas in the West. The saying, 'One thing leads to another', is in fact a pithy summary of Dependent Origination!

But let us take a loose example. A young man sees a shiny sports car. It inspires strong feelings in him – he imagines the elation as he drives down the road at 100mph with the hood down, the wind streaming through his hair, a pretty girl beside him. Desire is born: he wants to possess the car. So he borrows the money to buy it. Once he has it, his life changes. He has to work harder in order to run and maintain the car and to pay back his debt. It is a struggle, but he is so attached to the car that he cannot bear the idea of losing it. Things get difficult, so he takes on extra work. Gradually stress and overwork undermine his health. He falls ill with a kidney complaint. A few years later he dies, which in due course occasions a new birth. All this happened, the Buddhist explanation would run, because he was deluded – he thought that true fulfilment lay in getting that sports car, whereas in fact doing so merely led to a series of escalating complications. The rebirth that results from his death will merely repeat a similar process until the lesson is learnt and a firm resolution arises to seek escape from the endless cycles of old mistakes.

THE TWELVE NIDANA

Within the life-span of any human being, twelve separate causally active links or 'nidana' may be discerned. They are:

1 ignorance, that wilful blindness that leads to
2 volitional action. Volitional action in turn generates
3 conditioned consciousness requiring
4 a vehicle or body (name-and-form) to carry it through the world. That body will have
5 doors and windows: the sense organs (the so-called six bases – that is, the five senses plus mind) upon which stimuli will impinge, thereby creating
6 sense impressions, which in their turn will generate
7 feelings that lead to
8 desire. Desire is a kind of intoxicant that makes us blindly cling to whatever we find desirable (and of course reject what we find repulsive). So
9 attachment is created, and that in turn triggers
10 becoming, from which comes
11 birth – and birth, as the Buddha never tired of emphasizing, inexorably produces
12 old age, death – and indeed all the 10,000 ills and sorrows that flesh is heir to.

KARMA

What force couples each link in the chain of Dependent
Origination, keeping the Wheel of Life in perpetual spin? The
answer is karma. The word has now penetrated the Western
consciousness, though, from the Buddhist point of view at least,
in somewhat distorted guise. It is often called the Law of Cause
and Effect, so it is about the consequences of actions of body,
speech and mind.

Any action that is willed, however subtly, by the person who
performs it will always produce a future 'ripening' and ultimately a
'fruit' of similar moral quality, because in the human sphere karma
operates in an ethical manner. So an unethical action will induce a
comeback of like kind in this life or some future rebirth; and the
same goes for morally good or indifferent actions that are willed
and freely undertaken. In the *Bible* it says something similar: that
we reap what we sow. If we want to progress spiritually, we should
be very careful how we speak and act, for there is no way we can
escape the consequences. As it says in the *Dhammapada*, a concise
and poetic early Buddhist text:

*'If a man speaks or acts with an impure mind, pain
pursues him, even as the wheel follows the ox
that draws the cart.'*

This teaching should not be used as a pretext for unkind
judgementalism, however. For instance, were someone to fall ill, a
censorious person might declare, 'Ah well, that's the result of past
karma. He's merely reaping what he sowed.' This, however, is to
ignore the fact that non-karmic forces are also in play. Our bodies,
being organic, are subject to growth and decay regardless of how
we behave. Various circumstantial factors also have a bearing on

how things turn out. In any case, who is it that performs an action? If ego is ultimately an illusion, there is no doer, just the deed. Where then does moral responsibility lie?

Moreover, nowadays scientists are discovering that laws – and, in Buddhist terms, karma is a law – only work up to a certain point. Beyond that anything can happen. So indeterminacy or uncertainty is built into the basic workings of the Universe.

REBIRTH AND DEATH

As must have become quite clear by now, Buddhism does not hold with nihilistic views of death. There is no yawning abyss of pure nothingness into which we finally disappear. There is just Samsara, the cyclic world-process – and escape from it.

Buddhists are often thought to subscribe to the idea of reincarnation. This is not strictly true. Reincarnation presupposes that some kind of enduring soul or essence, something with unchanging personal imprints, commutes from body to body down through the marches of time. As we have seen, however, the Buddha denied the existence of any soul that might reincarnate. What he did admit of was something slightly different, which we might call rebirth. This maintains that there is a causal connection between one life and a subsequent one. Nothing is handed on in the transaction, however; the following life is a completely new one. But the form it takes is conditioned by the previous one.

The odds in favour of a human rebirth, from where

LEFT THE IDEA OF REBIRTH APPEARS IN BUDDHIST BELIEFS. HOWEVER, THE CONCEPT OF A SOUL THAT REINCARNATES IS DENIED.

alone escape from Samsara is possible, are said to be very slender. For example, If a blind turtle swimming in a vast ocean came up for air once every 100 years, what would be the likelihood of it putting its head through a golden yoke floating on the surface? So, if we are favoured with a 'precious human rebirth', we should take care to put it to good use in the interests of achieving liberation, otherwise we may be dispatched to the other grim 'destinations' – the hell realms, the realm of the hungry ghosts and so forth – and circulated there for aeons before we get another chance.

THE BARDO

In Tibetan Buddhism we find a detailed analysis of the states that arise in the bardo, or intermediate state, that intervenes between one life and another. The bardo is a terrifying phantasmagoria in which all kinds of spectres, gods, demons and other apparitions loom up before the bewildered disembodied consciousness traversing it. Wonderful 'luminosities' appear too, the first of which is the true Dharmakaya wherein lies liberation, but the consciousness traversing the bardo will usually be too confused to see them for what they are and will instead be swept onwards towards rebirth, which will take place within a maximum period of 49 days.

If a human rebirth is to take place, the future parents will be seen making love, lust will arise and the consciousness will try to interpose itself but find its way barred. The annoyance it then feels will be the seal of its conception.

CHANGE AND IMPERMANENCE

The Buddha stressed the dynamic nature of existence. This resonates with the ideas of some early Greek philosophers, such as Heraclitus, who maintained that 'All is flux' and 'You can't step into the same river twice.'

DESIRE

If the basic project of mainstream Buddhist practice is to unmask the ego illusion for what it is, one of the main prongs of attack is directed against desire. Desire is a poison, a disease, a madness. There is no living in a body that is subject to desire, for it is like a blazing house.

Now, desire lives and grows by being indulged. When not indulged by the application of ethical restraint and awareness, on the other hand, it stabilizes and begins to diminish, though this is not an easy or comfortable process, for the old urges clamour for satisfaction for a long time.

This kind of practice, of course, cuts directly against the main currents of modern consumer society, where desire is energetically

ABOVE A DETAIL FROM THE WHEEL OF LIFE. THE COCK, SNAKE AND PIG SYMBOLIZE DESIRE, AVERSION AND DELUSION.

encouraged and refined to new pitches and variations by the powerful agencies of marketing and publicity. But it also cuts against the more moderate desires – for family, wealth, sense-pleasures and so on – sanctioned in simpler, more traditional societies, including the one into which the Buddha was born. We can never be at peace while desire is nagging at us.

The flip-side of desire is aversion, a pushing away of that which we dislike as opposed to a grasping onto things we like. Aversion too must be put to rest.

Desire, aversion and their bedfellow, delusion, are the basic faults or frailties of character that drive us through the painful cycles of samsara. They are symbolically represented at the very hub of the Wheel of Life by a cock, snake and pig, all chasing each other and biting each others' tails in an unbreakable circular chain.

Now, all this sounds like common sense. Yet there is something about our minds and emotions that kicks against the idea of change. We are forever trying to break the dynamic world-dance, which is a unity, into separate 'things', which we then freeze in the ice of thought. But the world-dance doggedly refuses to remain fragmented and frozen. It swirls on, changing from moment to moment, laughing at all our pitiful attempts to organize and control it.

In order to live skilfully, in harmony with the dynamic Universe, it is essential to accept the reality of change and impermanence. The wise person therefore travels lightly, with a minimum of clutter, maintaining the proverbial 'open mind' in all situations, for he or she knows that tomorrow's reality will not be the same as today's. He or she will also have learnt the divine art of letting go – which means not being attached to people and possessions and situations, but rather, when the time for parting comes, permitting that to happen with grace.

HIGHER QUALITIES AND VIRTUES

Through taking the medicine that the wise doctor, the Buddha, prescribes – that is, through regular, balanced practice, usually over a fairly extensive period of time – many of the complicated problems that arise in life sort themselves out quite organically.

NIRVANA

The end of the path is likened in the early scriptures to the blowing out of a candle when there ceases to be fuel to keep it alight. This is nirvana. Identification with a self has ceased; indeed all urge to exist as a person – or to exist at all – has ceased. Desire and aversion have been pacified. Delusion has been replaced by clarity. At the micro level, the agitation of the dharmas has completely calmed down. Cyclic existence, birth and death, are transcended.

We must be careful not to understand this as sheer nothingness – or as a super transcendental something. It is beyond birth and death, existence and non-existence – and utterly beyond the power of the mind to know or of words to tell. We are assured, however, that it is the greatest bliss. Life in the body may still continue, and teaching may take place too – as in the case of the Buddha – but, ultimately, there is a further and equally ineffable transition at physical death. This is Parinirvana.

Of the Buddha's own final passing or Parinirvana, it is written in the *Majjhima Nikaya*:

> '*As a flame blown out by the wind*
> *Goes to rest and cannot be defined,*
> *So the wise man freed from individuality*
> *Goes to rest and cannot be defined.*
> *Gone beyond all images –*
> *Gone beyond the power of words.*'

Time and energy are at the same time freed for actively urging moral qualities such as patience, kindness, resolution, sympathetic joy for the successes of others, compassion for their suffering, and so forth. There is also more latitude for study and meditation.

As practice deepens over time, more specialized qualities will arise, including the higher form of wisdom we mentioned earlier. This enables the practitioner to see things as they really are, clearly, no longer through the distorting lenses of desire-based fantasy, projection and so forth.

As the process proceeds towards its culmination, detachment from both the world and the self advances. The clamour of urges within, the ripening of old karmic seeds, dies away until finally the practitioner is capable of such dispassionate acceptance of all the vicissitudes of life that even death ceases to frighten him.

DEVELOPMENTS IN MAHAYANA BUDDHISM

CHAPTER FOUR

As the Buddha said that all things were subject to change, it was quite consistent with basic principles that later generations of Buddhists should modify, restate and develop his teachings. In this chapter we will look at the most important developments that took place after the rise of the Mahayana. I want particularly to examine the reformulations of the anatman teaching, which many regard as the key teaching that distinguishes Buddhism from other Indian religious systems.

We tend today, of course, to separate Buddhism from the other Indian traditions, as though it had an autonomous life of its own. However, Buddhist thought and practice influenced, and in turn were influenced by, those of other non-Buddhist Indian schools.

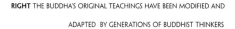

38

The anatman teaching was originally very much a reaction against the notion of atman, which is quite central to mainstream brahmanical religion. There exists, so brahmins and rishis (visionaries) believe, an Ultimate Reality or Self that they call Brahman, which can be found, not in some heavenly sphere, but in the heart of man, in which case it is called atman or the self. Actually there is no difference between Brahman and atman. The Self and the self are one.

The great rishis and yogis of the *Upanishads* stressed the unknowable nature of Brahman/atman. The best that they could do was to describe it in negative terms: Neti, neti ('Not this, not this'). The problem is, of course, that the thinking mind cannot let things rest. It will always conspire to trap them in the net of thought and describe them through the medium of words – even when warned not to do so. So gradually the idea of atman began to degenerate. Images and ideas were projected onto the blank screen of that great mystery – until it was a mystery no more.

The Buddha's mission was therefore essentially a reformist one. He wanted to purify atman of all those projections and restore its unknowableness. So, when he taught anatman, he was not asserting that there is no atman, no self (and hence no Self – no Ultimate Reality), as indeed many Buddhists have thought. Rather he meant that anything you think or say about atman is not atman. Atman is beyond all words and ideas. You cannot grasp it with the thinking mind. But perhaps you can purify and open yourself in order that it can fill you. Then you can be it.

Even the Buddha's formulation of the anatman doctrine, then, insofar as it is itself verbal-conceptual, cannot be perfect or definitive. Not surprisingly, therefore, not long after his death, slight distortions of the teaching began to creep in. With the rise of the Mahayana, therefore, new attempts were made to revitalize and restore the teaching to its original purity. In the process, as we shall see, the whole thing goes through a 180 degree shift, from negative formulations to more positive ones.

Indeed, we can trace shifts within the Buddha's own presentation. For instance, in *The Greater Sutta on the Destruction of Craving*, the Buddha sharply rebukes Sati, the fisherman's son, of the notion that 'consciousness (vinnana), not anything else, continues through life and from life to life,' this consciousness being 'what speaks and what feels and experiences the fruits of karma, good and bad.' The truth, the Buddha maintains, is that consciousness only arises in dependence upon the 'bases of consciousness' (ayatanas). Visual consciousness, for instance, only arises in conjunction with the sense of sight and visible objects. In the *Brahmajala Sutta*, on the other hand, the Buddha talks of 'consciousness which is characterless, unending, everywhere shining'. So in one case he seems to be denying that Ultimate Reality is pure consciousness, whereas in the second he appears to be admitting just that. Also, in the *Udana*, he

SHUNYATA

With the rise of the Mahayana, we find the Anatman Teaching reformulated in the concept of Shunyata ('Emptiness'). This Emptiness is not pure nothingness, of course; nor is it a kind of transcendental something. Rather it is a medicine to remedy the compulsive illusion-making habits of our minds, particularly their tendency to think of persons and things as separate, self-created and self-sustaining. Shunyata indicates, therefore, not the presence of something but rather a resounding lack or void, specifically a lack of inherent existence or 'own nature' (svabhava). This goes as much for dharmas, those ultimate essences of the world-process, as it does for people and things. In Abhidharma there is a general tendency to think that dharmas are somehow real, though not to the extent of possessing atman. In the Mahayana, however, dharmas are decreed unequivocally to be empty, along with everything else. Even Emptiness is ultimately empty!

talks positively of an 'Unborn, Unbecome, Unmade, Unconditioned', without which there would be no escape from all that is born, become, made and conditioned.

It would be wrong to see these things as simple inconsistencies. As the Buddha was a pragmatic teacher, his pronouncements were not meant to be definitive statements of truth but, rather, were shaped to suit the needs of the moment and the individuals that he was addressing. Sati was probably rather stuck on the idea that consciousness was Reality. The Buddha merely wanted to open his mind up again.

THE BODHISATTVA

As well as dissipating delusion, an understanding Shunyata (*see* box, p.40) is said to produce a de compassion (karuna) for the suffering of sentien beings. Compassion means 'to suffer with' – to actually share and feel the sufferings of others as though they are one's own. Obviously a breaking-down of those psychological boundaries that divide 'I' from others has taken place here.

In Mahayana teaching, compassion is thought to lead to a deep resolve to fulfil the goals of the spiritual life in order to help others to become free – particularly free from suffering. This is technically called bodhicitta ('Enlightenment mind') and its presence elevates a person to the status of a bodhisattva ('Enlightenment being').

RIGHT THE BODHISATTVA SEEKS ENLIGHTENMENT NOT FOR HIMSELF BUT FOR THE SAKE OF OTHERS. EVERYTHING HE DOES IS FOR ALTRUISTIC REASONS.

To become a bodhisattva one must already be well-advanced along the path. One must have fully understood the Buddha's teachings on karma and rebirth, Dependent Origination and so forth, had insight into Emptiness and felt the stirrings of deep compassion. In some texts, it is stated that some advanced bodhisattvas have actually attained Enlightenment; that is they are buddhas, no less. In others, however, it is suggested that they 'postpone' their own Enlightenment. Mostly, however, the term is clearly meant to signify someone who is a buddha-in-the-making, motivated altruistically rather than selfishly.

A fine impression of what it practically means to try to live the bodhisattva life is given by the Indian teacher Shantideva in his classic poem, *Bodhisattvacharyavatara* 'Guide to the Bodhisattva's Way of Life'. An enormously high degree of idealism and earnestness is required, such as one would expect to find extremely rarely, if at all, in our contemporary world.

42

To begin with, Shantideva is smitten with honour at the dire implications of life in Samsara. At any moment, one can be led away to the torture chamber or struck down with disease. The body is 'like an object on loan for but a minute', and when the 'frightful messengers of death' call, which can be at any second, it avails one nothing to have riches, reputation or loved ones. One quits this existence utterly naked and alone: 'Who can afford me real protection from this great horror?' he cries with very real anguish.

There is real protection, and a way of salvation – the way of the bodhisattva, in which resides an 'ocean of virtues'. Shantideva determines to follow it and be the doctor, medicine and nurse 'for all sick beings in the world until everyone is healed'. Thus bodhicitta (*see* p.41) is awakened and, seeing that a selfish orientation, far from achieving the happiness and satisfaction it seeks, merely perpetuates suffering, he surrenders it. Repenting wholeheartedly of all his former sins, he determines to bind the crazy elephant of the mind. For there is 'nothing to fear but the mind'; it is the origin and source of all evil actions that cause hellish suffering. He will therefore examine his mind before doing or saying anything and, if he finds his motivation tainted, will 'remain like a piece of wood'.

He will also be open and at times 'be the pupil of everyone' – excellent advice! Conscious too that one moment of anger can destroy the good generated by wholesome deeds performed 'over a thousand aeons', he will practise patience. If someone hurts him, he will reflect that this is just the ripening of his own past karma, and bear no malice. Indeed he will 'be happy to have an enemy', for it affords opportunity to practise patience and so assists his practice. He will also restrain his sexual passions.

The bodhisattva will consciously develop enthusiasm to counter any disposition to laziness that might impair his practice. Then, 'by seeing the equality of self and others' he will give up all 'self-cherishing' and 'practise that holy secret: the exchanging of self for others'. He will actually conceive of others as 'I', as his own self, their bodies as his body, and take to himself their suffering – though, of course, through his mastery of wisdom ('those who wish to pacify suffering should generate wisdom,' he tells us, devoting a whole chapter to the subject), he knows that in the final analysis there is no 'I', hence no owner of suffering. Building up his generosity, he will

43

also give everything away, even his own flesh. And all this will be done, not out of some drab sense of duty, but with actual joy. He can never do enough for others. He would even enter the deepest hell to alleviate their pains.

LEFT MANJUSHRI, THE BODHISATTVA OF WISDOM AND ONE OF THE BENIGN DEITIES. HIS SWORD SLICES AWAY FALSE VIEWS AND DELUSIONS.

THE BODHISATTVA PATH AND ITS PERFECTIONS

The various bhumi or stages on the Bodhisattva Path are fully charted in the Mahayana, as are the perfected virtues (paramita). There are six or sometimes 10 of these 'paramita':

1 dana (giving)
2 shila (morality)
3 kshanti (patience)
4 virya (effort)
5 dhyana (meditation)
6 prajifa (wisdom)
7 upaya (skill-in-means)
8 pranidhana (resolution)
9 bala (strength)
10 jnana (knowledge).

The development of these virtues corresponds to a 10-stage Bodhisattva Path. As set out in the *Dashabhumika Sutra*, the stages are called:

1 Pramudita (the Joyful)
2 Vimala (Purity)
3 Prabhakari (Refulgence)
4 Arcishmati (Blazing)
5 Sudurjaya (Difficult to Conquer)
6 Abhimukhti (Presence)
7 Duramgama (Far Going – beyond this stage it is not possible to 'backslide')
8 Acala (Immoveable)
9 Sadhumati (Good Mind)
10 Dharmamegha (Cloud of the Dharma), the very apotheosis of bodhisattvahood, where they will protect and enlighten all beings, be omniscient, 'lords of the ten powers' and so on.

Finally, in true bodhisattva style, Shantideva dedicates all merit (good karma) that might accrue to him to the liberation of all beings everywhere, and hopes that they will 'obtain an ocean of happiness and joy'. For the true bodhisattva's compassion is never limited to a few chosen beneficiaries. It goes out equally to the whole world, like the warmth of the sun. The same qualities of goodwill, friendliness and harmlessness are bestowed upon all, without distinction, 'as if they were his mother, father, son or daughter'.

THE ABSOLUTE AND THE RELATIVE

Mahayana teachers do not deny that there is a conventional world, only that this world is not what we usually take it to be; that is, real (permanent, self-sustaining, containing separate entities and so on). This world has its own truth too, but it is a relative truth that is, by its very nature, compromised, not perfect. There is another frame of reference that is not compromised, however. It accurately reflects reality. The absolute truth that obtains here is called paramartha satya. Worldly or relative truth is called samvriti satya. We could call them profound truth and superficial truth. They correspond to two perspectives: the transcendental (lokottara) and the worldly or relative (laukika).

45

PRAJÑAPARAMITA, 'PERFECTION OF WISDOM'

The first major Mahayana teaching to emerge was the Prajñaparamita or 'Perfection of Wisdom' (the so-called 'Wisdom that Has Gone Beyond'). Here we find a number of difficult texts of varying length. One very brief one, for instance, maintains that the whole teaching can be summed up in the letter A (Skt. Ah). Another takes 100,000

ABOVE PRAJÑAPARAMITA, THE GODDESS OF
WISDOM. THE PRAJÑAPARAMITA, OR
PERFECTION OF WISDOM, WAS THE FIRST
MAJOR MAHAYANA TEACHING TO EMERGE.

verses to present it. *The Heart Sutra* and *The Diamond Sutra* are the most well-known and among the most concise texts.

All the texts are declaimed from the lokottara or transcendental point of view. That is, from a position of absolute non-duality, beyond all discriminative thought and verbal constructions. Viewed from this sublime vantage-point, which is really no different from that of Enlightenment itself, there is no Buddha and no Enlightenment, no defilements and no purification, no production (of dharmas) and no extinction, no karma and no consequences of karma. There are no beings to be saved, therefore no bodhisattvas to save them. Form merges with emptiness, Samsara with Nirvana.

How can such things be? Well, the Buddha could not think 'I am the Buddha', for instance, for that would mean he had in his mind the idea of a person who possessed buddhahood. Being a buddha, he is at one with buddhahood; there is no duality. Therefore, for the Buddha there is no Buddha. Likewise 'Enlightenment' is an idea that only occurs to those who are not Enlightened. Indeed, they are a long way from it. It is 'those who do not consider whether they are far from Enlightenment, or near it' who are truly on course. And again, 'Nirvana' and 'Samsara' are only concepts in the minds of those who discriminate. For those who do not discriminate (that is, buddhas and bodhisattvas), Samsara and Nirvana become exactly the same.

So all terms, including spiritually prestigious ones such as 'buddha', 'Enlightenment', 'bodhisattva', 'karma' and 'dharma', are just conventional constructions. Buddhas and bodhisattvas use them as skilful means to help suffering beings – though of course in an ultimate sense there are no beings and no suffering. Thus buddhas and bodhisattvas regard those whom they help as no more real than an army of phantoms conjured up by a skilful magician.

What then is the Prajñaparamita mode like? It can be compared, the texts say, to the vacuity and purity of space. The buddhas and bodhisattvas who 'course in it' take their stand nowhere and in nothing, neither in the conditioned nor the unconditioned. They seek no psychological supports, yet their position is diamond-solid. It will not crumble like Samsara and all its creations. For Samsara, it is continually emphasized, 'has no inner core':

> *As stars, a fault of vision, as a lamp,*
> *A mock show, dew drops, or a bubble,*
> *A dream, a lightning flash, or cloud,*
> *So should one view what is conditioned.*
> *(From the short Prajñaparamita texts,*
> *translated by E. Conze.)*

47

The Prajñaparamita exults in its own transcendental perspective and brings it poetically alive, while at the same time conspiring to strip us of all affirmations, all mental/verbal constructions, and drive us into the arms of that marvellous Beyond.

THE 'MIDDLE WAY' SCHOOL

Tradition has it that the amorphous teachings of the Prajñaparamita were systematized by a sage named Nagarjuna (second century CE), the seminal master of the Madhyamaka or 'Middle Way' school. Highly celebrated, Nagarjuna is sometimes characterized as a second Buddha.

Though some have disputed his historicity, written records say that Nagarjuna came from south Indian brahmin stock. He initially mastered magic, which he successfully used to make himself

LEFT NAGARJUNA WAS A SECOND CENTURY SAGE, WHO, ACCORDING TO LEGEND, PRODUCED THE PRAJÑAPARAMITA TEXTS.

invisible so that he could seduce the women in the local palace. However, when three of his friends were caught and executed, the perils of lust were forcibly brought home to him and he hastily embarked on Hinayana Buddhist training. Later he graduated to the Mahayana. He subsequently wrote texts, notably the *Mulamadhyamaka-karika* 'Middle Way Verses'; there are suggestions too that he was responsible for the composition of some Prajñaparamita texts. He masterfully championed the Mahayana in open debate with the devotees of other Buddhist and Hindu schools, such as the Samkhya, Vaishesika and Nyaya. Highly venerated, he spent his later years in a monastery built for him by a patron-king, and ended his life by his own hand. His chief disciple was another south Indian brahmin named Aryadeva.

Nagarjuna brought to Mahayana Buddhism, not some creative new philosophical position, but a critical method that, if properly applied, would expunge all views and opinions by showing their ultimate absurdity, thereby at once restoring the mind to its native Prajñaparamita mode, free of all dualistic thought formations. As he himself says at the conclusion of the *Mulamadhyamaka-karika*:

'I reverently bow to the Buddha who, out of compassion, has taught the true doctrine in order to relinquish all views.'

So this is a philosophy that arrives at no conclusions. It in fact puts an end to all speculation and rumination – or, put another way, it probes the ultimate limits of what can be meaningfully thought and said.

NAGARJUNA'S TETRALEMMA

Nagarjuna's method is described as dialectical: that is, it exploits the quirky, dualistic nature of language to turn all propositions on their heads. He uses various devices to this end, notably his famous tetralemma, by which a simple proposition may be reduced to four logical forms:

1 A
2 not-A
3 both A and not-A
4 neither A nor not-A.

To take a concrete example:

1 Everything is real
2 Everything is unreal
3 Everything is both real and unreal
4 Everything is not real and not unreal.

49

Nagarjuna also draws a parallel between Shunyata (Emptiness) and Pratitya Samutpada (Dependent Origination). In Nagarjuna's view, the importance of the latter is that it points up the dependence or relativity of all things in the conventional world. They are like the parts of a cathedral, all helping to maintain and support each other, so that if one is taken away the whole structure will collapse. Seeing dependence and relativity in this way is to see Shunyata and be thereby liberated. This liberation depends, then, upon a change of perception and knowledge, nothing more. The world does not become another world, for there is no separation between Samsara and Nirvana – 'the limit of Samsara is the limit of Nirvana'.

The influence of Nagarjuna and his school was enormous. Stringent Madhyamaka became the dominant philosophy in Tibet and remained so down to the time of the Communist takeover in 1959. It was also successfully transmitted to both China and Japan, and is at present being enthusiastically studied in the West.

YOGACARA

Although Nagarjuna wanted to show the futility of all views, both positive and negative, the ruthless nature of his method – one writer calls it a kind of philosophical sadism – has a tendency to nihilism. As a counter to this negative disposition there later arose a sub-school, the Svantantrika of Bhavaviveka and his colleagues, which took a more positive line. An even more positive line was taken by the masters of the Yogacara or Vijnanavada school, who asserted the primacy of consciousness. The objects of the external world are not 'real' or external at all, they argued, but transformations of consciousness or mind. In support of this thesis they pointed to the fact that things can appear in the mind when there is no 'external' object present – in a dream, for instance, or through the practice of imaginative visualization.

In other schools this is known as the teaching of Citta-matra or 'Mind Only'. In the West it is called Idealism, the notion that only minds and mental events exist, which opposes Materialism, the notion that only matter exists. The most distinguished proponent of Western Idealism is Bishop Berkeley (1685–1753), who maintained that to exist is to be perceived and that perceptions are just ideas in the mind. It might therefore be asked: if a tree, for instance, only exists while it is being perceived, what happens to it when there is no-one around to perceive it? Does it politely fade away? No, the worthy bishop would reply, it continues to exist even then – because all things are contained in the mind of God.

According to Buddhist writings, the seminal master of the school was a shadowy figure named Maitreyanatha. His more famous successors were two brothers, Vasubandhu and Asanga (both fourth century CE), who were natives of Gandhara.

Asanga first studied with masters of the pre-Mahayana Mahishasaka school. However, after spending 12 years in meditative retreat and feeling that he had gained nothing from the experience, he became profoundly disillusioned. Asanga then met a mangy dog, which inspired him with deep compassion. This was fortunate, for the dog was the Coming Buddha, Maitreya, in disguise. Maitreya promptly initiated the kindly Asanga into the Mahayana and dictated many texts to him, including the *Yogacarabhumi* 'Ten Stages of the Yogi's Path'.

Vasubandhu, meanwhile, had attached himself to the Sautrantika school, though he spent four years in Kashmir studying the Abhidharma system of the Vaibhashikas, a group of

Sarvastivadin scholars. At first he was contemptuous of his brother's new-found wisdom, a system, he declared, 'so difficult and burdensome that it could only be carried by an

RIGHT THE PHILOSOPHY OF YOGACARA STATES THAT OBJECTS EXIST ONLY IN THE MIND OR CONSCIOUSNESS OF AN INDIVIDUAL.

elephant'! Vasubandhu was to rue those caustic words. Hearing some texts read, he was later so illuminated that he wanted to cut out his own tongue. He then read through one vast sutra in a mere 15 days and nights, sitting in a bath of sesame oil to keep awake. Afterwards he became a great writer of Mahayana texts and commentaries himself, an expert debater, the founder of monasteries, nunneries, dharamsala (guest-houses) and hospitals, as well as tutoring the son of the Emperor Govindagupta.

According to the Yogacara view, mind is subject to three levels of possible modification. There is citta, which includes the six kinds of sense consciousness; and there is manas, the 'I' consciousness. These develop from alaya-vijnana, the so-called 'store consciousness' level of mind, a kind of subconscious in which the experiences of the past are stored as 'seeds' (bija) of future experiences. This produces a momentary stream of consciousness whose waves subside when all the seeds are exhausted.

Yogacara was not just a speculative philosophical school. As its name suggests, it was based on yoga practice. So it was said of Vasubandhu that he was 'attempting to explain that which is beyond the power of words to convey, and which came to him by the mysterious way of profound meditation.'

The philosophical aspect is therefore just upaya, skillful means, to point the devotee towards a profound insight that can only be gained through actual practice. This is the so-called 'revolution at the basis' (ashraya-paravrtti). When a person finally sees that external objects are just projections of his own consciousness, he realizes that there is no object to be seized and no person to seize it. This leads to the Path of Insight, which gives access to an ultimate state where, all the seeds of the alaya-vijnana having been exhausted, perfect quiescence in a deep samadhi of pure consciousness supervenes. This is devoid of all content, beyond the subject-object dualism, and as such is identical with the Dharmakaya.

In the words of the master, Vasubandhu:

'When consciousness does not apprehend
any object-of-consciousness, it is situated in
'consciousness-only',
for with the non-being of an object apprehended,
there is no apprehension of it.
It is without citta, without apprehension,
and it is super-mundane knowledge;
It is revolution at the basis, the ending of the two
kinds of susceptibility to harm.
It is the inconceivable, beneficial, constant ground,
not liable to affliction,
bliss, and the liberation-body called the
dharma-body of the Sage.'
(From Seven Works of Vasubandhu,
translated by Stephen Anacker.)

TATHAGATAGARBHA

The positive implication that the central mystery of man and the Universe enshrines a 'something' rather than a 'nothing' is also to be found in the Tathagatagarbha doctrine, which is expounded in texts such as Ashvaghosa's Awakening of Faith in the Mahoyana, the Shurangama Sutra and the Tathagatagarbha Sutra. This suggests that each person is a receptacle or womb containing the potentiality or embryo of buddhahood. It only needs the right practice to remove the covering defilements and expose this eternal Reality.

This of course is to take Buddhism perilously close to an atman teaching, a fact not lost on some apologists, who asserted that the doctrine had only been taught as an upaya or skilful means for luring benighted Hindus, hopelessly addicted to the idea of atman, into the Buddhist fold.

ZEN

Such rarefied philosophies as we have been briefly discussing of course stand in stark contrast to the noble silence that the Buddha is said to have maintained when plied with questions of a metaphysical or speculative nature. However useful, they only amount to head knowledge; and it is in fact very easy to be immensely learned about Buddhism (or anything else for that matter) in a scholastic sort of way and be utterly unable to make the quantum leap to actualising the teachings – making them live in our own daily lives. To know all about Buddhism and to be a living example of it are in fact two very different things.

The Zen school arose in China in the sixth century CE precisely to grapple with this problem. There were in the monasteries and temples Buddhist monks and nuns who had accumulated a great deal of head-knowledge. They had also steeped themselves in

ABOVE JAPANESE ZEN BUDDHIST MONASTERY. ACCORDING TO ZEN PHILOSOPHY, THE GREAT QUESTIONS IN LIFE MUST COME FROM WITHIN OURSELVES.

Buddhist morality and the monastic code of discipline. But they were stuck and could not make the necessary quantum leap. What the early Zen masters provided, therefore, were powerful new methods – many of them iconoclastic by conventional Buddhist standards – for pushing those practitioners beyond thought and discipline, up to a whole new octave-level where they could directly see into the great mystery of things for themselves. Generally, the Zen school looks positively at the great mystery at the heart of things. 'What is it?' is one of the classic questions that practitioners are urged to address with unremitting energy. Yet the early masters would brook no answer that smacked, however slightly, of conceptual thought. They demanded one that was existentially authentic: that came directly from the heart, from the human centre that enshrines the great mystery of man and the Universe.

All Buddhist teaching, then, insofar as it bears upon that great mystery, is a kind of circumambulation around it. Different doctrinal approaches are formulated to suit the unique circumstances of specific times and situations. Yet in the end we must let go of all thought and verbiage, let go of everything in fact, so that the great mystery may live through us.

MORALITY

In contemporary Western culture, morals have become decidedly unfashionable. It is just not hip and sexy to keep to the rules and be good. This is largely because our own religious traditions have stagnated and their ethical bases degenerated into rigid codes hostile to change, development and healthy self-expression. On the other hand, living religious traditions, vitalized at source, produce dynamic and relevant morals, and in the past they have provided the springboards for great cultural advances.

We humans are essentially moral beings. We only become immoral in degenerate social conditions that stunt proper development. We *want* to be ethical. Indeed we need to be, for morals are the forms that mould the expression of our living energies, enabling them to manifest their highest potential: highest in terms of most beautiful, noble, creative and harmonious.

So as a first practical step on the Buddhist path, we try to put our lives in good order. Just doing this in itself makes us feel better, less ill at ease with ourselves and less at odds with the world at large. We become more peaceful, more trusting, and that in turn causes good things to happen back to us – and to those around us.

Ideally, ethics should spring naturally from the heart, but in the first instance, at the beginner's stage, most of us need some kind of code to guide us. The basic code that Buddhism offers is Pancha Sila or the Five Precepts.

THE FIVE PRECEPTS

1. KILLING

Firstly, there is the principle to refrain from killing any living being. This of course includes the almost universal injunction against the murder of other human beings; but it also extends to include all kinds of other beings as well – animals, birds, fish and insects – for they too are spiritual beings like us, possessing the potential for spiritual growth, which includes of course the possibility they might themselves sometime attain human rebirth. Animals may also be regressed humans, for according to the Law of Karma it is possible for humans who have behaved badly to be reborn in that state.

To be true to this principle and not collude in murder after the event, many Buddhists become vegetarians, though this is not obligatory. Early Buddhist monks, for instance, being beggars, could accept meat that was put into their begging-bowls. They were only required to reject it if they knew that its butchering had been done specifically for them. Tantrists naturally have a different attitude. Meat actually figures as a sacrament in some rituals.

LEFT THE BUDDHIST PRINCIPLE TO REFRAIN FROM KILLING ANY LIVING BEING MEANS MANY FOLLOWERS ADOPT A VEGETARIAN DIET.

2. THEFT

The second principle is to refrain from taking that which is not given. That is, stealing and its variants – including 'liberating' articles from shops, 'borrowing' books and failing to return them and all kinds of sharp practice, including many that have become socially acceptable in our go-getting society. In general, obtaining anything for oneself in ways that cause others to suffer is not morally sound, even if technically no law is breached.

3. SEX

The third principle is to refrain from irresponsible sexual activity: that is, activity that hurts others in any way. As the strongest passion to which we are prone, sex is always highly-charged karmically. It can cause all sorts of things to happen, not least that a new life enters this world. It must therefore be regulated, but at the same time it cannot be safely repressed.

All sexual activity is, of course, proscribed for Buddhist monks and nuns, but it is understood that lay people will have sex lives – though, of course, this is not obligatory! Celibacy is quite a healthy state, if again it does not involve repression; that is, a denial or thwarting of the libido whereby it is thrust below consciousness.

ABOVE SEXUAL ACTIVITY SHOULD TAKE PLACE WITHIN A RESPONSIBLE AND LOVING RELATIONSHIP.

On the matter of sex, however, it must be said that generally Buddhism is not very positive. The Buddhist sutras and other works speak very disparagingly of this very natural instinct, basically because it was seen as the primary means whereby people become entrammelled in family life, which affords restricted opportunities for spiritual practice.

In general, then, the Buddhist message would seem to be: if you are serious about living the spiritual life, it is best to have transcended sex. The exception again of course is Tantra, which characteristically takes its stance at the opposite pole and seeks to integrate sexuality – indeed to use sexual energy as a means for gaining Enlightenment.

4. SPEECH

The penultimate principle is to refrain from harmful misuses of the faculty of speech. These include lying, slander, malicious or idle gossip, misrepresentation, blackmail and so forth. Obviously these can cause pain to others and create disharmony.

5. DRINK AND DRUGS

The final principle is to refrain from ingesting substances that befuddle consciousness. Not only do these lead to heedless activity – many crimes, including crimes of violence, are committed under their influence – but they also impede awareness and, as we shall see in the next chapter on meditation, the development of awareness or clear-seeing is essential.

Drink and drugs are also often avenues of escape from the dark and difficult things of life, including our own problems. Indeed, problems cannot be effectively solved while a person is addicted to them. So there are many good reasons for not taking drink or drugs – or at least to the extent where they begin to impair awareness.

Of course, the monastic codes make drink and drugs absolutely off-limits for monks and nuns, but Tantra yet again has its own antinomian attitude to these things, and in lay circles in the West today things also differ from the patterns established in the East. In our cold, northerly lands, ale has traditionally been a staple beverage, spirits a comforter and wine a sacrament. Many Western Buddhists, therefore, are not averse to a moderate amount of social drinking – moderate being the operative term here – though many others at the same time prefer to abstain completely.

ABOVE DRINKING ALCOHOL IN MODERATION IS ACCEPTED BY MANY BUDDHISTS IN THE WEST.

Something must also be said about drugs. Since the 1960s, many genuine spiritual searchers have experimented with consciousness-raising drugs such as LSD, cannabis, peyote and mescalin, and claim to have received profound experiences under their influence. Whether such experiences are really spiritual has been questioned; and in any case they do not produce lasting changes – only sustained practice can do that. There are also identifiable dangers connected with specific drugs, and the fact that they are illegal surrounds them with a paranoid ambience. However, no conclusive evidence for their spiritual relevance or irrelevance exists as little dispassionate research has as yet been done.

RIGHT LIVELIHOOD

Additional to the moral precepts outlined above, we find mention of Right Livelihood in the Noble Eightfold Path, an early graduated scheme of the way to Enlightenment. This means earning our living in ways that do not harm, deprive or exploit other people, animals and the environment. The modern obsession with economic growth has, however, produced a culture where anything goes as long as it makes money.

LEFT NURSING IS A NON-HARMFUL WAY TO EARN A LIVING.

We can see that implicit in all five precepts is the age-old Indian principle of ahimsa: not harming – either others or oneself. We can safely extend this to the environment, the world as a whole and even to space. Nothing falls outside the sphere of our moral responsibility.

Of course, any harmful action will, according to the Law of Karma, refract back on the being that perpetrates it; and morally wholesome actions conversely induce positive come-back. But the Five Precepts should not be regarded as grave and rigid laws. The Buddha did not want to make us guilt-ridden or into rigid fundamentalists who grasp the letter of the law but miss the spirit. A lot of disharmony and suffering can be generated by stickling demands for strict adherence to principle, whereas a little good-hearted flexibility can make for more harmony and less complication.

The precepts, then, are in the nature of ideals or guidelines, to be used with flexibility and good sense. If we fail to live up to any of them, we should not torment ourselves with visions of hellish punishments. Rather we should learn from our failure and resolve to do better in future. Moral perfection is therefore something towards which we all-too-fallible humans aspire; it is not something we can hope to achieve totally and at once.

Nor should morality be used as a stick with which to beat others. If we have any degree of self-knowledge, we know a little about our own failings and so will not be too hasty in making judgements. The urge to judge in any case usually stems from projection of our own dark side. This causes us to see other people's failings glaringly well, for they are precisely the failings that we cannot bear to contemplate in ourselves! So the moderately wise person attends to his or her own faults, attempting to rectify them, and does not preoccupy him or herself overly with the faults of others.

Finally there is also this to bear in mind. The real aim of spiritual practice is not to serve the self-centred ego. Quite the opposite; it's about becoming free of the ego's endless concern with self-interest. Now, most immorality is ego-serving and operates directly at the expense of others and the Universe in general. Morality is therefore a primary curb on the ego and a first step towards liberation from that whole nexus of compulsions.

MEDITATION

CHAPTER SIX

Whaat is meditation? The truth is, we live our lives in a kind of waking dream. We are only hazily aware of what is really going on both outside and, even more so, inside ourselves. Every chance stimulus – every random meeting or event, every vagrant emotion, mood, impulse and so on – just sparks off a more or less automatic reaction. It needs a vital shock, like a stark confrontation with death, to jerk us awake. Then for a moment the scales of semi-sleep, subjectivity, projection and fantasy fall from our eyes and we see the world as it really is.

Meditation is about developing that kind of acute awareness all the time. And it means doing so without becoming attached to the objects of observation out of desire, or rejecting them from aversion. It means becoming the dispassionate watcher, the one who knows: becoming buddha, in fact. Buddhism traditionally has a word for meditation – smrti: Mindfulness.

RIGHT MEDITATION HELPS US TO UNDERSTAND THE TRUE NATURE OF THE WORLD.

MINDFULNESS

The basic form of meditation that the early texts describe the Buddha as teaching is not sitting meditation, but something to be done by a monk as he 'fares along', going about his normal business. It consists of the specific applications of Mindfulness, described by the Buddha in the *Satipatthana Sutta*:

> *'There is this one way, monks, for the purification of beings, for the overcoming of sorrows and griefs, for the going down of sufferings and miseries, for realizing Nirvana; that is to say, the four applications of mindfulness. What are the four? A monk fares along contemplating the body in the body, ardent, clearly conscious of it, mindful of it so as to control covetousness and dejection in the world; He fares along contemplating the feelings in the feelings, the mind in the mind, and the mental objects in the mental objects, ardent, clearly conscious of them, mindful of them so as to control covetousness and dejection in the world.'*

Although it is emphasized in this text that Mindfulness should be established 'precisely to the extent necessary just for knowledge, just for remembrance' and 'independently of and not grasping anything in the world', its application should be wide and deep and along prescribed lines. For instance, when in contemplation of the body, the practitioner should not be merely aware of his present posture or any

RIGHT AS YOU PASS A CEMETERY MEDITATE ON THE NATURE OF
THE BODY – THAT IT IS SUBJECT TO DEATH AND DECAY.

action he may be performing; he should also at appropriate times reflect upon the nature of the body – the fact that it is like a skin bag containing various impurities, organs, bones and so on. Special emphasis is laid on the gruesome aspects of the physical body, and if he passes a cemetery the practitioner is urged to reflect that his body too is of the same nature as those that now lie there 'swollen, discoloured, decomposing'. In this way, attachment to the body is undermined.

The benefits to be obtained from this practice are very high: 'either profound knowledge here-now, or, if there is any residuum remaining, the state of non-returning' (that is, the state of a being who rises to a higher world and reaches Nirvana without being reborn in this world again).

How to Practise Basic Meditation

Most practitioners sit on the floor on a small, plump cushion. They assume the classic cross-legged lotus or half-lotus position. If this is not possible, a straight-backed chair will do. The important thing is to keep the back straight (though not stiff or rigid) and the head balanced on the upright neck. The hands should be laid loosely in the lap, one lying inside the other or holding the other firmly. The eyes are then half closed and the arrow of attention turned inwards.

LEFT ADOPT A LOTUS OR CROSS-LEGGED POSITION FOR YOUR MEDITATION PRACTICE. MAKE SURE THAT YOUR BACK IS STRAIGHT.

Now, letting go of all active preoccupations (planning, problem solving, scheming, fantasizing and so on), we come fully into the here-now. Just allow yourself to relax alertly into the aware state. This state is not something we have to create. It is the ground of our being; all we have to do then is allow it gently to come into its own. So there should be no goal-oriented striving or forcing, only the exertion of sufficient energy to prevent us lapsing into an empty sleep-like or day-dreaming state.

Next, steer awareness towards a particular object. Usually the rise and fall of the breath is recommended. Watch how it passes in and out of the nostrils, or watch the rise and fall of the diaphragm. Or you can concentrate on the 'fire-field' of the tanden or area some five centimetres below the navel – whatever is most comfortable.

Of course in the beginning – and indeed for a long time afterwards, for that matter – it is very difficult to keep awareness on target. The mind, accustomed for so long to its own wayward habits, will tend to wander away and be caught and excited by any thought that happens to stray into its ambit – and so off into the endless labyrinths of rumination.

But now you can make a start at breaking this vicious cycle. Gradually you will experience moments when the mind is marvellously calm and clear, the heart at peace – but only temporarily – the old turmoil will relentlessly return, time and again. You must not be discouraged, however, or think you are a bad meditator. Meditation is one area where judgement or competition is right out of place. Instead just go back to the basic breath-watching practice and patiently persist with it. Also do not allow yourself to become attached to those wonderful moments of calmness and clarity, or contrive to reconstruct them. Attachment and striving will only inhibit their return. All you can do is go on, doing the best you can.

Because most of us do not normally like to confront ourselves honestly, when we begin to open up the mind in meditation a great deal of repressed or forgotten material will often rise into consciousness, sometimes disturbingly. If this happens, you should again observe that material, not getting caught up with it on one hand but certainly not trying to suppress or violently destroy it on the other. For here you have a rare chance to undergo very effective psychotherapy. If you hospitably allow it, however dark or disturbing it may be, to enter consciousness and rest there, in full awareness, it will in time fade away quite naturally. Then you will learn the great truth that your biggest bogies – your deepest fears, guilts and pains; your most distressing problems – are no more substantial than the morning dew. Awareness, like the sun, will evaporate them.

THE FIVE HINDRANCES TO MEDITATION

There are in fact traditionally said to be five 'hindrances' which impede progress in meditation. They are: sensual desire, ill-will (or aversion), laziness, restlessness and worry and doubt.

ZEN MEDITATION

The Zen school might be called the meditation school par excellence. Ostensibly disparaging scriptural learning and other practices (such as performing rituals, reciting the scripture and so on), it emphasizes direct seeing into one's own nature. The early Chinese Zen masters do not especially recommend sitting meditation; direct seeing can be accomplished – and sustained – in everyday life. However, later Chinese and Japanese Zen stress the importance of zazen or sitting meditation – and lots of it, both by day and at night.

Legend has it that Zen originated in India, but really it came into its own in T'ang dynasty China. Of the so called 'Five Houses' that flourished then, only two have survived to the present, but these have been successfully transmitted to the West via Japan. They are the Lin-chi (Japanese, Rinzai) and the Ts'ao-tung (Japanese, Soto).

Soto Zen meditation is usually practised facing a blank wall. The internal method is essentially formless. The Japanese master Dogen, who transmitted the teachings of the school from China to Japan, declares that zazen is not learning to do concentration. It is not introspection. It is not thinking of good or bad. It is not a conscious endeavour of any kind. There should not be expectations. One should not even desire to become a buddha. He advises the meditator to just:

RIGHT A MANDALA IS USED AS A FOCUS FOR MEDITATION. IT IS NORMALLY CIRCULAR IN DESIGN, AND ENCLOSES A SQUARE.

> *Sit solidly in meditation and think not-thinking.*
> *How do you think not-thinking? Nonthinking.*
> *This is the art of zazen.*
> (from *Rules for Zazen*, trans. D Welch and K Tanahashi
> in *Moon in a Dewdrop: Writings of a Zen Master*,
> ed. K Tanahashi)

In this respect, practice and realisation are not separate. Just to sit is to be a buddha.

Meditation in the Rinzai tradition (*see* pp.93–96), on the other hand, is rather more militant. Practitioners sit in straight lines, facing each other. They begin perhaps with a breath-watching or counting practice to bring about calmness and concentration. Then they traditionally apply themselves with concerted effort to koan practice.

KOAN RIDDLES

Koan riddles (Chinese, kung-an) are generally based on the records of real life situations in which early masters enlightened their students. In Sung dynasty China, as Zen began to lose its original flair and vitality, these were collected in great anthologies such as the *Blue Cliff Record* and the *Gateless Gate*. These formalized riddles, now having something of the significance of precedents in case law, are still handed out to Rinzai Zen practitioners today. Pondering them long and deeply, the student will attempt to give an 'answer' to the teacher, usually in Japan called a roshi or 'old master', in the course of regular interviews (sanzen). The roshi will then judge its authenticity. Any 'answer' that smacks however slightly of conceptualization or phoney contrivance will be ruthlessly rejected. If, however, the devotee comes up with an acceptable answer, he or she may well be adjudged to have had a genuine breakthrough or satori.

However, that is just the beginning. More work must be done to deepen understanding. In other words, once a degree of calmness, clarity and concentration has been produced, the koan is an extremely active device for continually throwing the student against the ultimate question of his own nature.

A classic account of intensive koan practice is given by Hakuin, the revitalizer of Japanese Rinzai Zen. At the age of 24, while staying at the Eigan temple, he grappled with the koan Mu ('No', 'Not') by day and night, forgetting both to eat and rest:

'Suddenly a great doubt manifested itself before me. It was as though I was frozen solid in the midst of a sheet of ice extending tens of thousands of miles ... To all intents and purposes I was out of my mind and the Mu alone remained ... This state lasted for several days. Then I chanced to hear the sound

ABOVE A SELF-PORTRAIT OF THE ZEN MASTER HAKUIN (1686–1769), SITTING WITH A HORSEHAIR FLYWHISK IN HIS HAND.

69

of the temple bell and I was suddenly transformed. All my former doubts vanished as though ice had melted away. In a loud voice I called: "Wonderful, wonderful. There is no cycle of birth and death through which one must pass. There is no Enlightenment to seek ..." My pride soared up like a majestic mountain ... Smugly, I thought to myself: "In the past 200 or 300 years no one could have accomplished such a marvellous breakthrough as this".'

(Zen Master Hakuin: *Selected Writings*, trans. P B Yampolsky, 1971.)

Unfortunately, his master dismissed all this as derived from study, not from the intuition.

'You poor hole-dwelling demon!' he jeered, much to Hakuin's chagrin.

Hakuin applied himself equally assiduously to another koan – only to achieve the same humiliating result. Then one day he took his alms-bowl to a nearby town and was beaten by a madman. Strange to say, this produced enlightening results: he penetrated the meaning of various koans that had hitherto puzzled him. But again the Master neither approved nor denied what he said, though he stopped calling him a hole-dwelling demon. Hakuin then went back to attend his old teacher, Nyoka, who was sick.

More breakthroughs followed, but it was not until he was 32, at the dilapidated Sham temple at Hara, that he at last perfected his understanding. Then he uttered a great cry and burst into tears, having come to the conclusion:

'Studying Zen under a teacher is not such a simple matter after all.'

TANTRIC MEDITATION

Buddhist Tantra aims at bringing about Enlightenment very
speedily by special yogic means. It is not, however, according to its
own teachings, suited to everyone. Only special candidates who
have already practised long and successfully gained deep insight
into Shunyata (Emptiness) as well as having developed a high
degree of bodhicitta qualify to practise it. Then they must forge a
connection with a learned guru, who will initiate them into the
mandala or sacred precinct of their chosen deity (yidam). The rite
of initiation (abhisheka) that the guru bestows allows the devotee to
perform a range of specialized rituals and practices (sadhana),
many of which involve working with dark aspects of the psyche.

LEFT A WRATHFUL
DEITY FROM THE
TANTRIC PANTHEON.

Herein lie special dangers, so both to protect the unwary from burning themselves and the teachings from being debased, Tantra is hedged around with a veil of secrecy, grave vows and other protections.

Buddhist Tantra possesses an extensive pantheon of yidam or deities. Some, such as Avalokiteshvara, the Bodhisattva of Compassion, his female Tibetan form of Tara and Mañjushri, the Bodhisattva of Wisdom, are benign. Others, such as Yamantaka, Mahakala and Chakrasamvara, are wrathful. All possibly developed from ancient non-Buddhist Indian deities. Chakrasamvara, for example, is a Buddhist transformation of Shiva, the Hindu deity of death and regeneration.

Insofar as Tantra involves meditation, it presupposes a solid basis in Mindfulness and Shamatha-Vipashyana. Given these, its own distinctive practices involve creative visualization. The devotee will learn, for instance, to create the form of his chosen deity out of the bija or seed mantra that embodies the essence of the deity, the bija being firstly created out of the Emptiness of his own mind. The mental image of the deity must be built up in very precise detail and full colour according to archetypal patterns.

The Tantric yogi aims to eventually acquire the enlightened qualities of his yidam – which are really his own innate enlightened qualities. While this might be quite understandable in the case of benign deities, it is perhaps far less easy to understand in the case of wrathful ones, which in traditional iconography are depicted as extremely macabre beings with bloodshot eyes and flaring fangs, sporting necklaces of skulls, carrying skull-caps and daggers and surrounded by wreaths of fire. Some couple passionately with their shakti consorts – a symbol of both the union of wisdom and skilful means, and of the bliss of the Enlightenment that union produces. For according to the Buddhist view, such dark and passionate energies, when purified, possess enlightened qualities.

FUTURE DEVELOPMENTS

At present most Western Buddhist meditators practise according to the time-honoured traditions of the particular Oriental school to which they feel drawn. There have, however, been fruitful experiments with combining traditional meditation methods and modern Western psychotherapeutic techniques. The latter are very good at dealing with blocks and problems frustrating development to the full ego stage – that is, the stage of mature autonomous individuality – while the Eastern methods serve very well in the 'transegoic' phases: The phases of consciousness beyond the 'I' stage.

A useful start has also been made, mainly in the US, in the serious academic study of different traditional methods and the psychospiritual world of consciousness in which they operate.

Finally, it is to be hoped that, as meditators become increasingly proficient, there will be a new phase of experimentation and innovation, perhaps with combinations of meditation techniques from different schools and traditions. This arguably more than anything else would be warranty of the continuing vitality of Buddhist meditation.

THE PRINCIPAL SCHOOLS AND TRADITIONS

CHAPTER SEVEN

THERAVADA BUDDHISM

Tracing its roots back to the seminal Sthaviravada school that arose in India after the Buddha's death, the devotees of the Theravada, or 'Way of the Elders', would argue that their tradition is the true repository of the teachings and practices propagated by the Buddha himself. In their eyes it therefore stands as a fixed pole of orthodoxy and tradition amidst the melée of 2,500 years of change and development. Others would, however, dispute this, arguing that the Theravada is itself a very much later development and that consequently the tradition can make no claims to special priority.

LEFT THERAVADA BUDDHISTS BELIEVE THAT THEIR TRADITION IS CLOSEST TO THE TEACHING OF THE HISTORICAL BUDDHA.

Whatever the truth of the matter, the Theravada survives today as a living tradition in Sri Lanka, Burma and Thailand, and it is from these countries that it has been transmitted to the West. The *Pali Canon* is still very much its scriptural foundation, and the Pali language rather than Sanskrit is used for chanting and other liturgical purposes. A lively tradition of Pali scholarship exists, also an active tradition of meditation. In the East, while the scholar-monks tend to gravitate to the larger temples and monasteries where facilities exist for their work, the dedicated meditators are more likely to seek out secluded places. These 'forests monks' may live in outlying monasteries or else alone in caves or huts similar in manner to the early Sangha (Community). Some wander from place to place, accepting whatever in the way of food or shelter may be offered to them – or not offered. This is regarded as a form of dhutanga or hard practice, and is considered to be particularly beneficial for shaking off the defilements.

As a sign of their renunciation of worldly values, monks and nuns shave off all their facial and cranial hair, and wear the traditional ochre or orange robe. Having committed themselves to a life of poverty and mendicancy, they have few possessions, but one essential is a bowl into which lay devotees may put food. They also vow themselves to chastity, and the most scrupulous will neither carry nor touch money. All strive hard not to be idle or to fritter energy away in self-indulgences, such as unnecessary sleep or gratuitous chatter. Bounded as they are at all times by their numerous precepts and rules, they have in any case to be constantly mindful of what they are doing and able to accept a very high degree of circumscription. Hierarchy is important too. When addressing those senior to them – that is, those who were ordained earlier than they were – monks should bow and generally show due respect.

At the British Theravadin monastery that I visit, the monks get up very early – at 4.00 am — and go to the shrine-room, where they chant for some time before the great gilded image of the Buddha, then sit in silent meditation. According to the rules, they are only allowed to eat between dawn and noon. They therefore have a simple breakfast of plain rice gruel and tea. Afterwards chores are done, and some monks will leave on the daily alms round, taking their begging bowls with them. As food donated by the laity is prepared in the monastery kitchen by lay-brothers (anagarika) and laity, this Oriental tradition might be thought unnecessary. However, it is maintained out of respect for tradition and also so that the community can keep in touch with the local people. The substantial meal of the day is duly taken before 12.00 noon, then there is a period of rest before the afternoon work-session begins. Tea is taken in the late afternoon, plus certain allowable 'medicines' such as cheese or black chocolate. Then at 7.30pm it is back to the shrine room for more chanting and silent meditation. At about 9.00pm monks and nuns are free to go to bed, but must be ready to rise again when the bell rings at 4.00am.

This austere daily routine goes on year in, year out, punctuated only by periods of retreat when the community draws together for more intensive practice. Some monks or nuns may also embark on solitary retreats, or go off on dhutanga – the 'hard practice' mentioned above, when they wander from place to place, usually in the West accompanied by a lay-brother or a layman. There may also be visits to schools, local Buddhist societies and other places to deliver discourses and/or lead meditation.

Within this particular community, any person wishing to take the robe has first to serve a probationary period of at least one year as an anagarika. He (or she) then shaves both head and face, dons a white robe and lives by eight precepts – that is, the Five Precepts (*see* pp.57–61) plus three additional ones: not to eat at wrong times; to refrain from dancing, singing, music, attending shows, wearing garlands and using perfumes and cosmetics; and not to lie on a high or luxurious bed. In addition, he or she will be encouraged to take on board some 75 rules of etiquette.

His term as an anagarika completed, a man may request to be given the monk's precepts – 227 of them in all, though only about 20 are of practical significance today – at a ceremony held before the annual

Vassa or Rains Retreat in a sima or consecrated space. He will then be able to wear the ochre (or orange) robe. A woman, on the other hand, cannot become a fully-fledged nun as the order of nuns has technically died out, but she may take the vows of a Dasa Sila Mata or 10 Precept Sister, which is what we mean by 'nun' in the present context. This is done at a ceremony in the shrine-room when she will exchange the white robe for a brown one. She is then bound by the eight precepts listed above, of which the seventh, concerning dancing, singing and so on, is divided in two, plus an additional precept prohibiting the handling of money, gold and silver. She will also take on numerous training rules. Four rules, known in Pali as Parajika Offenses, are considered especially grave and anyone transgressing them would be expelled from the order and not allowed to rejoin. These concern sexual intercourse, deliberate killing, deliberate stealing and claiming to possess paranormal powers. All the rules are rehearsed by the whole community twice monthly on Uposatha days.

A life circumscribed by so many rules, which drastically curtail personal liberty and self-expression, might seem a very bleak prospect. Many who have actually lived it, however, report that after initial struggles they actually begin to feel more free – free in particular from the burden of the self and its endless conflicts and demands. This leads at times to the welling up of great joy and a sense of serenity. Of course, if the life does not prove suitable, a monk or nun may leave at any time by handing their robes back to their preceptor. However, as this is regarded as a serious step they will be counselled first and asked to pause before making a final decision. Leaving does not, however, debar anyone from seeking reordination at a future date.

The traditional relationship between Theravadin monastics and laity is one of useful symbiosis. The monastery is the spiritual focus of the locality in which it is situated. Monks live and practise there, and the laity may come to stay for a period of retreat or just for a brief visit. Uposatha days – hill and half moon days – and festivals draw large crowds of lay devotees, who come with dana (gifts), including food to offer to the monks and nuns. Afterwards there may be a communal meal and there is usually much conviviality. There will be a certain amount of ritual too: chanting from the Pali scriptures is usual, the delivery of a blessing, a discourse from the abbot, perhaps a period of silent reflection and the recitation of the Five Precepts. The Three Refuges may also be taken when, led by the monastics, the laity will chant the Pali formula:

'Buddham saranam gacchami;
Dhammam saranam gaccham;
Sangham saranam gacchami.'

– repeated twice more with the prefix 'dvutiampi' first and then 'tatiampi'. Taking refuge in this way is an important rite, affirming or reaffirming one's faith in Buddha, Dharma and Sangha. It is thus a kind of Buddhist confirmation. It is also open to different levels of interpretation: for instance, on one level one may be affirming one's faith in the historical Buddha, Shakyamuni, but on another one may be affirming faith or confidence in one's own Buddha-nature: the buddha within.

Special ceremonies are also carried out at monasteries to celebrate rites of passage – birth, marriage and death. The principal Theravada festivals include the celebration of the Buddha's Birth, Enlightenment and Parinirvana – called Wesak in the Sri Lankan tradition, Vaisakha Puja in the Thai – on the full moon day of May; and Kathina in October or November, which celebrates the ending of the three-months Rains Retreat when monks withdraw into their monastery for intensive practice. At Kathina, the laity bring special gifts for the Sangha, notably cloth for robes.

There is a school of thought that maintains that real practice is possible only if one ordains into the Sangha. However, in recent years there have been successful attempts in the West to establish intensive lay practice on the basis of a particular meditation technique.

Especially influential have been the Burmese 'noting' and 'sweeping' systems pioneered by Mahasi Sayadaw and U Ba Khin, and successfully propagated to Westerners by Joseph Goldstein, Sharon Salzburg, S N Goenka and others.

TIBETAN BUDDHISM

The Tantric Buddhism of Tibet could not stand in stronger contrast to the Theravada. When travellers familiar only with the Southern School first encountered it they thought that if indeed it was Buddhism then it could only represent a fall from the high spiritual standards set by the Buddha.

To walk into a Tibetan temple is to be confronted by raw primary colours – red, blue, green, mustard – the mingled aromas of strong

79

ABOVE TIBETAN TEMPLES ARE FOUND IN SECLUDED LOCATIONS HIGH IN THE MOUNTAINS.

incense and butter lamps, the benign and wrathful deities depicted on scroll paintings hanging on the walls or painted on the walls themselves, and a rich array of gilded figures and votive objects. If there are lamas present, one may hear the monotonous, guttural drone of their chanting, periodically augmented perhaps by the cacophonous clash of cymbals and the wailing of thigh-bone trumpets and other instruments. Here are suggestions of magic and mystery that resonate with something suppressed and half-forgotten in the depths of our being. Small wonder, then, that Tibetan Buddhism is probably the most popular form of Buddhism in the West today, barring the fast-growing Nichiren cult.

Their seclusion on the Roof of the World enabled the Tibetans to preserve the Mahayana and Tantric Buddhism of India for over a millennium and to create a uniquely rich spiritual culture. Unfortunately in 1950 the Chinese Communists felt the need to 'liberate' these people from the thrall of Western imperialism. Despite the fact that there were virtually no Westerners – and certainly no imperialists – in Tibet at the time, the Chinese went ahead and became imperialists themselves, taking over the government of what had hitherto effectively been an autonomous nation, colonizing it, plundering its mineral and natural wealth and making the Tibetans themselves virtual aliens in their own land. The Tibetans voted with their feet against this 'liberation', and when the Chinese finally – and bloodily – completed their takeover in 1959, tens of thousands fled to exile in India. The virtual destruction of Buddhism in Tibet was completed during the Cultural Revolution (1966–1976).

Yet these violent and destructive events did have one positive outcome – they made the spiritual riches of Tibetan Buddhism accessible to Westerners for the first time. After 1959, lamas – including HH the Dalai Lama – began to visit the West. Tibetan Buddhist centres were set up, the first being Samyé Ling, established in the lowlands of Scotland in 1967 by two Karma Kagyu lamas, Akong Rinpoche and Trungpa Rinpoche. Others soon followed, and today we can claim that four major schools are well-established on Western soil.

THE NYINGMA SCHOOL

The Nyingmapa, or followers of the tradition dating back to the first transmission of Buddhism to Tibet, tend to be rather more anarchic than the Sarmapa ('New Ones'). The Nyingma School is less inclined to monasticism and decidedly more inclined to magic. Its followers particularly venerate the Tantric adept Padmasambhava (Guru Rinpoche).

Padmasambhava originally came from Oddiyana in what is now the Swat Valley of Pakistan. Having overcome the occult forces hostile to it, Padmasambhava successfully transmitted Buddhism to Tibet in the seventh century CE. This great siddha did not apparently deliver all his teachings at that time, however, but cunningly hid some – the so-called termas or 'treasures' – in both geographically-locatable places as well as 'in mind', so that they could be discovered later when people would be better qualified to understand the deep wisdom they contained. The general Nyingma classification of teachings tends to be slightly different from that of the other schools and it opts for a six-fold rather than a four-fold classification of Tantras.

The last head of the school, HH Dudjom Rinpoche, a married lama, died in France in 1987.

THE SAKYA SCHOOL

There was a time during the 12th and 13th centuries when the high lamas of the Sakya school, which takes its name from its great monastic headquarters in southern Tibet, were vassal kings of Tibet under Mongol overlordship. Before its fortunes fell into decline, the school also enjoyed great spiritual influence. The most important doctrinal and meditational cycle of the Sakya school is a piece of writing known as *The Path and its Fruit*, a systematic presentation of both Sutra (that is; pre-Tantric) and Tantric teachings credited to the ninth century Indian adept Virupa and based on the *Hevajro Tantro*. This has both an exoteric and an esoteric presentation.

81

According to Ngakpa Jampa Thaye (David Stott):

'The philosophical viewpoint that informs The Path and its
Fruit is the notion of the inseparability of Samsara and Nirvana
...It is said: "By abandoning Samsara one will realize Nirvana."
Mind itself, the union of Luminosity and Emptiness, is the root
of Samsara and Nirvana. When obscured it takes the form of
Samsara and when freed of obscurations it is Nirvana.
The key to Buddhahood, the ultimate source of benefit for
all beings, lies in this realization.'

By following this path one can apparently attain Enlightenment in a single life. The Sakya school has now two sub-sects, the Ngor and the Tshar. Its present supreme head is HH Sakya Trizin, who was born in Tibet in 1945 but is based in northern India.

THE KAGYU SCHOOL

Practical mysticism rather than bookish scholarship characterizes the Kagyu school – 'Kagyu' literally meaning 'Transmitted Command'.

Written records tells us that one of its seminal Indian masters, Naropa (1016–1100 CE), devoted a great part of his early life to scholarship, eventually attaining high office at the great monastic university of Nalanda. A vision of an old crone then revealed to him that the knowledge he had acquired was merely dry intellectual stuff, not the transrational knowledge of the heart. The effect was traumatic; it drove Naropa to the verge of suicide. He was saved, however, by the discovery of his own guru, Tilopa (988–1069 CE), who had himself received instruction from the primordial buddha Vajradhara. Over a 12-year period, Tilopa put Naropa through a gruelling course of Tantric training.

After the suppression of the first transmission of Buddhism to Tibet by the evil king Langdarma, a generation of Tibetans collected gold and departed to India to obtain teachings and texts. These were the lotsawa ('translators'). One of them, Marpa (b. 1012), travelled three times and studied with Naropa as well other great masters. Among the teachings he received were the so-called Six Yogas of Naropa and Mahamudra. The Six Yogas include Tumo, which, as a side-effect, generates such a degree of physical heat that wet towels placed on a yogi's body in icy conditions will dry out very quickly. Mahamudra ('Great Seal'), meanwhile, is a very high practice giving direct access to the luminous Dharmata or ground of being. On returning to Tibet, Marpa settled down to an ordinary life as a farmer and family man.

Marpa's most famous disciple and heir to the Kagyn lineage was Milarepa (1052–1135), who, because he had foolishly dabbled in black magic, had also to be put through an extremely rigorous course of training. Never ordaining as a monk and avoiding institutions, Milarepa became the much-loved prototype of the freewheeling yogi who pursues his own spontaneous spiritual path in lonely places. He gained many wonderful powers as a result of his austerities and was able on one occasion to defeat a priest of the Bön religion in a contest of magic for the possession of Mount Kailas, the great sacred mountain in Western Tibet. Milarepa was also a poet.

Milarepa's most influential disciple was the 'Doctor of Takpo', Gampopa (1079–1153), author of the classic text, *The Jewel Ornament of Liberation*. From his disciples stem three Kagyu sub-schools, the Drug, Drigung and Karma. The last bead of the Karma Kagyupas, the 16th Gyalwa Karmapa, died in Chicago in 1981, but not before seeing his school successfully transmitted to the West. The credit for this is due in large measure to the work of Chbgyam Trungpa Rinpoche (born 1939), who, having fled Tibet and received a Western education at Oxford, helped set up a Kagyu centre in Scotland before moving to the US, where he founded the extensive Vajradhatu organization with headquarters in Boulder, Colorado. Gifted with unique talents as a Dharma teacher, plus a fair salting of fleshly frailties, controversy – even notoriety – dogged Trungpa for much of his short-lived teaching career.

THE GELUG SCHOOL

As its name – Gelug means 'virtuous' – suggests, this began as a reform movement initiated by Tsongkhapa (1357–1419); also known as Jé Rinpoche), a pious monk from north-eastern Tibet. Wishing to see Tibetan Buddhism restored to the pristine purity of its Indian sources, Tsongkhapa attacked what he believed to be heretical views, notably those of the Jonang school, whose followers had reputedly adopted a form of soul or atman doctrine. He also stressed the importance of a basis of ethics and, for monks, the monastic virtues (strict celibacy, abstention from intoxicants and so forth), and he encouraged study so that practitioners might obtain a clear intellectual understanding of the nature and aim of the Buddhist path. He felt particularly strongly that a firm grounding in the Sutra teachings should be obtained before any attempt was made to negotiate the heady world of Tantra.

In his *Lam Rim Chenmo* (*Great Exposition of the Graduated Path* [to Liberation]), Tsongkhapa outlines preliminary practices relevant to the Sutra level of training. These include development of faith in the guru or teacher and correct motivation; meditation on impermanence and the preciousness of human birth, on karma and sufferings of beings in the six destinations of existence; and practices aimed at the accumulation of merit and the elimination of 'black karma'. The practitioner is urged to investigate and test the teachings at every stage, as a goldsmith assays gold, in order to ascertain, through reasoning, whether they are truly valid. In his *Ngag Rim Chenmo* (*Great Exposition of the Mantra Path*), meanwhile, Tsongkhapa deals with Tantra, which, as in all Tibetan schools, is the apogee of spiritual practice.

Gelugpas wishing to follow the path of philosophical study to the highest levels follow a special programme of higher studies. A monk completing this and passing his monastic examinations will be awarded the title of geshe. One Westerner has to date been awarded a geshe degree, but many others have ordained as monks and nuns and trained in Gelug monastic centres in both the East and the West.

The time-honoured system of debate is still practised in both the Tibetan and English languages; also reflective meditation on the stages of the Graduated Path and the visualization techniques of the Tantric system. Many of these Gelug centres are directed by Tibetan monk-lamas and, although the aim is to preserve the purity of the tradition, many spiritual directors nowadays incorporate elements of Western culture, such as psychological approaches. The needs of lay people, who may practise to as high a level as they are able within the constraints of their everyday lives, are also catered for at many of these centres.

Tsongkhapa's chief disciples founded the Gelug school, which enjoyed both spiritual and temporal preeminence in Tibet from the 16th century down to 1959. It was the Mongols, the original patrons of the school, who bestowed the title 'Dalai Lama' on its third head, 'Dalai' meaning 'Ocean (of Wisdom)', and also retroactively on his predecessors back to Gendun-drup, putative nephew and disciple of Tsongkhapa. The present incumbent, the 14th, is the monk Tenzin Gyatso. He was born in 1935 in eastern Tibet but presently living in Dharamsala, his 'capital-in-exile' in the foothills of the Indian Himalaya.

85

The 14th Dalai Lama's great spiritual qualities, his warmth and cheerfulness, and the way in which he has led his people through one of the most difficult periods of their history, always advocating a non-violent response to Chinese violations in Tibet, won him the Nobel Peace Prize in 1989. He is, along with the Fifth and the 13th, one of the great Dalai Lamas of all time.

RIGHT THE CURRENT DALAI LAMA, THE 14TH, IS NOTED FOR HIS WARMTH OF SPIRIT AND HIS COURAGE IN ADVERSITY.

THE LAMA IN TIBETAN BUDDHISM

It is hard to overestimate the importance of the lama in the Tibetan tradition. The word means a guru or teacher, who may be either married or a celibate monk, though not all monks teach. The commentary to Tsongkhapa's *Foundations of All Excellence* explains that 'the very root to Enlightenment is the practice of reliance on a spiritual teacher.' It goes on:

'Having realized that the spiritual teacher is the root of all excellence, by continuous effort of body, speech and mind, develop great faith that recognises his knowledge and does not observe in him the slightest fault. Remember his vast kindness with deep gratitude, and honour him; make offerings to him, respect him in body and speech, and strive to put his teachings into practice.'
(From The Jewelled Staircase, Geshe Wangyal.)

Whilst most teachers live impeccably and practise what they preach, some are unfortunately discovered to have feet of clay. Asked about this, HH the Dalai Lama told an audience in London in 1985:

'It is said that it is important for a student, prior to making a Dharmic connection with someone as a teacher, to understand what the qualifications of a guru or lama are in accordance with what is set forth in the Vinaya (that's to say, the Discipline), what's set forth in the Discourses [Sutras] and what's set forth in Tantra. Then it's also said that a person who wishes to become a teacher must understand what these qualifications are and work at fulfilling them. Then in the Mantra [Tantric] system there

> *is a mode of procedure for highly-realised adepts whereby they engage in activities that are not usually allowed. Effectively, this is when they have achieved stability. What is meant by stability? It is when the adept has the capacity to actually overcome in others the loss or lack of faith that such activities might usually cause... However, if a lama does not have this capacity and we think, "Oh, these are the grand activities of a high lama," then we are in a difficult situation and must make up our minds as to how to proceed.'*

ZEN

The legendary origins of Zen go right back to the Buddha. Because of the limited understanding of the majority of his followers, the story goes, Shakyamuni was forced to teach in words and concepts. There were higher teachings, however: non-verbal ones involving the direct transmission of understanding from the heart of the teacher to that of the disciple, completely by-passing the head. Such a teaching took place when Shakyamuni simply held up a flower, the monk Kashyapa got the message and an exchange of knowing smiles signified a profound spiritual transaction had taken place.

The school is said to have been transmitted to China in the sixth century CE by an Indian monk named Bodhidharma. He was presented to Emperor Wu of Liang, who asked about the meaning of the Buddha's teachings. 'Great emptiness; nothing at all holy,' Bodhidharma replied, implying that endowing temples and performing other pious works would not lead to realization, only to the accumulation of good karma. The Emperor then asked, 'Who is facing me?', to which Bodhidharma replied, 'I don't know.' Leaving the Emperor nonplussed, Bodhidharma then departed and spent many years meditating before a blank wall at the Shaolin temple, a place still famous for its martial arts connections. Later he reluctantly began to teach.

Legends aside, Zen – Ch'an in Chinese – is really a Chinese development, incorporating elements of the indigenous traditions, notably Taoism. It properly came into its own with the sixth Patriarch, Hui-neng (638–713 CE), an illiterate who was suddenly enlightened on hearing the *Diamond Sutra* recited while selling firewood. He then went to study at the temple of the Fifth Patriarch, Hungjen (601–674), and was put to work on the threshing floor. When Hungjen wished to appoint his successor, he invited his students to show the depth of their understanding by submitting poems. All the monks deferred to the head monk, Shen-hsiu (c. 600–706), who reluctantly pinned up a poem in which he compared the mind to a bright mirror from which the dust (of thought) had constantly to be wiped. The next night the 'barbarian' from the threshing floor submitted a second poem in which he pointed out that, since the Buddha-nature is always clear and bright, 'where is there room for dust?' This proved to Hung-jen that Hui-neng did indeed possess a deeper understanding of Zen that Shen-hsiu, but he dared not openly confer the transmission on him as he knew it would infuriate the other monks. He therefore gave him the patriarchal robe privately and told him to leave – quickly.

According to tradition, the rivalry between Hui-neng and Shen-hsiu split Ch'an into two schools. The Southern School of Hui-neng favoured the notion of sudden Enlightenment, while the Northern School of Shen-hsiu favoured the gradual variety. Further sub-divisions occurred and subsequently Five Houses and Seven Schools emerged, all basically propagating the teachings of the Southern School. Of these only two survive in the modern world – the Lin-chi and the Ts'ao-tung, which were successfully transmitted to Japan. Zen was also transmitted to Korea, where it is known as Son, and to Vietnam, where it combined with Pure Land in a successful local synthesis.

CLASSIC CHINESE ZEN

Very little Chinese Zen remains today. In any case, the golden age of the school was over a millennium ago, during the T'ang dynasty (618–907 CE). Afterwards it became formalized and lost much of its original vitality, though it survived – and indeed more successfully than the other schools – and still occasionally produced an outstanding master, such as Hsü-yün, who, when he died in 1959, was reputed to be 120 years old.

But what was the vintage Ch'an of the T'ang dynasty like? After centuries of immersion in the teachings brought from India, Chinese Buddhists at last felt confident to make their own unique approach to the core of the Buddha's spiritual project. It was clear that intellectual study could only produce dry head-knowledge, not the direct trans-rational 'un-knowledge' of the heart. So the early masters laid primary emphasis upon direct seeing into the self nature and improvised ingenious ploys to achieve this – shouts and clouts, bizarre behaviour and repartee:

89

LEFT CLASSIC CHINESE ZEN BUDDHISM EMPHASISES THE IMPORTANCE OF SEEING INTO ONE'S OWN NATURE.

> *'One day as the master [Pai-chang] was walking*
> *along with Ma-tsu [his teacher], they saw a flock of*
> *wild ducks fly by. The ancestor said, "What is*
> *that?" The master said, "Wild ducks." Ma-tsu said,*
> *"Where have they gone?" The master said, "Flown*
> *away." Ma-tsu then grabbed the master's nose;*
> *feeling pain, the master let out a cry. The ancestor*
> *said, "Still you say, Flown away?"*
> *At these words the master had insight.'*

This is Enlightenment, not at some indefinite time in the future, but right here, now, without any shilly-shallying. For in Ch'an the highest realization is not to be postponed until we are completely purified or have gathered a plethora of scriptural knowledge or clocked up a record-breaking score of meditation hours. To strive for goodness or knowledge, even to seek Enlightenment or to become a buddha, is indeed to pile up further obstructions to attainment. It is like running all over the world looking for a pearl that is fixed to one's forehead.

As Huang-po told an audience, quoting sutra: 'What is called supreme perfect wisdom implies that there is really nothing whatsoever to be attained.' (from *The Zen Teachings of Huang-po*, translated by John Blofeld).

If this is so, how then is one to practise? According to Pai-chang, like this:

> *'When things happen, make no response:*
> *keep your minds from dwelling on anything*
> *whatsoever: keep them for ever still as the void*
> *and utterly pure (without stain): and thereby*
> *spontaneously attain deliverance.'*
> *(from The Zen Teachings of Hui-Hai on*
> *Instantaneous Enlightenment,*
> *translated by John Blofeld.)*

And Huang-po:

> *'I advise you to remain uniformly quiescent and above all activity. Do not deceive yourselves with conceptual thinking, and do not look anywhere for the truth, for all that is needed is to refrain from allowing conceptual thought to arise'.*

The field of Zen, therefore, is mind – our own minds; for the One Mind or Buddha Mind and our own minds are not essentially different. According to Pai-chang, 'The nature of mind has no defilement; it is basically perfect and complete in itself.' Our problem is that we sully it with our greed and desire; with discriminative thoughts of good and bad, like and dislike, existence and non-existence; with our concern with past and future – but most of all with our attachments. If we let it all go, mind returns to its native purity, free of obstructions like a shining mirror that can reflect whatever passes into its boundaries because it is empty. Precisely this is buddhahood. But it is not to be confused with blank tranquillity. That is yet another trap. Ch'an Enlightenment leans neither towards activity nor to quietude. The mind should abide nowhere and in nothing – not even in not-abiding!

Classic T'ang dynasty Ch'an did not emphasize formal sitting meditation as an end in itself. Rather, they taught that sitting stilled both mind and body and thereby created the 'inner potentiality' for direct insights to arise in everyday life. Furthermore, many now take the view that the differences between the various sub-schools were not particularly marked.

JAPANESE SOTO ZEN

T'sao-tung Ch'an was transmitted from China to Japan by Eihei Dogen (1200–1253), where it became known as Soto Zen. it was transmitted to him by Ju-ching, the abbot of T'ien-t'ung Mountain, a stickler for monastic discipline and single-minded intense sitting meditation. Ju-ching was the one truly impressive Ch'an master that Dogen came across during his spiritual wanderings in 'Great Sung' (China).

Dogen had become a monk at the unusually early age of 13, the deaths of his aristocratic parents having forcefully impressed the truth of impermanence upon him. Later he developed a 'great doubt' while studying at the famous centre of the Tendai school on Mount Hiei. In the *Mahaparinirvana Sutra* it was stated that 'all beings everywhere have the Buddha-nature'; but if this is so, Dogen pondered, why do we bother to practise at all? This set him off in search of an authentic teacher.

Dogen attained a Great Enlightenment during 1225, when Ju-ching shouted, 'When you study under a master, you must drop the body and the mind; what is the use of single-minded intense sleeping?' Two years later he returned to Japan 'empty handed' – that is, not bearing scriptures or relics but being himself a living exemplar of the Buddha's teaching. He spent the rest of his life teaching, firstly in Kyoto and later away from metropolitan temptations and pressures in a remote and comfortless province, where he established the temple of Eihei-ji. Having been advised by Ju-ching to live in steep mountains and dark valleys, avoiding cities and villages, and not to approach rulers or ministers, Dogen likewise urged his own followers to drop the pursuit of wealth and fame, those perennial hindrances to the spiritual life, and instead to dedicate themselves wholeheartedly to practice. He was a fairly prodigious writer too, his great work being *Shobogenzo* (*Treasury of the True Dharma Eye*).

Central to Dogen's teaching is the importance of intensive sitting meditation and the notion that we are not potentially but actually buddhas when we sit. Practice and realization are one and immediate. Implicit in this is rejection of the notion that in the current dark age realization is impossible. He also evolved some original ideas of his own, notably that the Buddha-nature is not beyond impermanence, it is impermanence. And, finally, though he taught both monks and laity, men and women, he believed very strongly in a sound monastic basis and worked hard to create that.

JAPANESE RINZAI ZEN

Lin-chi Ch'an was transmitted to Japan, where it became known as Rinzai Zen, by Myoan Eisai (1141–1215). Like Dogen, who came after him, when Eisai returned from China he ran into trouble with the powerful Tendai sect, which succeeded in getting the Zen sect prohibited by imperial edict. Unlike Dogen, however, Eisai was prepared to compromise, and both Tendai esotericism and Zen meditation were practised alongside each other in his temples. Though he was in no doubt that Rinzai Zen represented the quintessence of the Buddha's Dharma, Eisai felt its hour had not yet come in Japan. Nevertheless, he laid a foundation upon which subsequent Japanese and Chinese masters could build.

Early Japanese Rinzai masters tended to go to Kyoto, the imperial capital, and Chinese masters to Kamakura, where the Shogunate was established in 1185. This was the real centre of power, for the rising samurai class had by now eclipsed the old imperial aristocracy. The samurai found Rinzai Zen very much to their liking, and a dynamic 'on-the-instant' warrior Zen evolved in Kamakura, which used, not

93

the classical formalized koan riddles, but ones improvised on the spot using an incident or situation with which the trainee was familiar. What, for instance, might a samurai do if, while getting naked

LEFT KIYOMIZU TEMPLE, KYOTO.
THE EARLY RINZAI MASTERS
CONGREGATED IN KYOTO,
THE IMPERIAL CAPITAL.

into his bath, he found himself surrounded by a hundred armed enemies? Would he beg for mercy or die fighting? How might he manage to win without surrendering or fighting?

After the initial vitality of the Kamakura period, Japanese Buddhism went into a long decline. Because it enjoyed the favour of the Shogunate, the Rinzai Zen sect survived most successfully of all the schools, and during the 14th and 15th centuries lavishly endowed temples flourished, notably the so-called Five Mountains in Kyoto, which are extensive complexes adorned with the finest works of art. Such places fostered that high aesthetic refinement we associate with the Zen arts.

However, the overall drift, both then and thereafter, was towards institutionalization, formalization and state regulation, and down to modern times there was little in the way of significant innovation or development, except in the lives and works of two masters, Bankei and Hakuin.

94

Bankei Yotaku (1622–1693) was one of those rare spirits who have the courage to find their own unique spiritual path, even if it means bucking against some of the hallowed conventions. His teaching sparkles with originality, and it was certainly highly effective in his own day, for huge crowds drawn from many different persuasions came to hear his discourses. At a time when Zen had become an élite preserve requiring command of classical Chinese and other recherché talents, Bankei was able to transmit its essence to ordinary people in terms they found accessible. He also had a gift for inspiring his listeners with confidence in their own spiritual potentiality. He even addressed 'mere women', telling them that they possessed the Buddha Mind just as men did.

Born into a samurai family, Bankei was something of a tearaway as a child; but then, in one of the Confucian classics, he discovered a reference to something called 'Bright Virtue'. This fascinated him to the point of obsession and he wandered far and wide in search of someone who could explain the meaning of the term to him. Unfortunately, the teachers he met were not of very high calibre, so he had to look for an answer within himself. Many years of intense, even desperate endeavour ensued and eventually his health began to crack. Then one day he flushed a gobbet of clotted phlegm from his throat and felt strangely refreshed. In the same instant he realized that – 'Everything is perfectly managed with the Unborn, and because up till today I couldn't see this I've been uselessly knocking myself out!' (*Bankei Zen*, Peter Haskel.)

This Unborn is, of course, the same 'Unborn, Not-become, Not-made, Not-compounded' that the sutras mention. It is also the pure, shining mind of the Zen masters. But unlike most other masters, Bankei came to the conclusion that it is not necessary to go through protracted rigours and austerities to discover it. Nor does he seem to have thought very highly of formal practice – he talks disparagingly of 'device Zen' that depends upon techniques. The monks in his monasteries did meditate but he did not lay heavy obligations or rules on them. The important thing is to discover the Unborn, and this can be done simply and directly, even by lay people. The trick is then to remain with it amidst the hurly-burly of everyday life. If thoughts arise, they should neither be suppressed nor indulged, for to be caught by them is to exchange the Unborn Buddha Mind for that of a fighting demon, a hungry ghost or some other tormented victim of bad karma. One should just remain detached and see that thoughts are transient illusions with no real substance. They will pass, leaving only the shining Unborn Buddha Mind – and in the marvellous, effortless functioning of this one can have complete confidence.

Hakuin Zenji (1688–1769) was a completely contrasting character who never lost faith in the rigours and austerities of hard practice and underwent them fully himself. Small wonder then that he spoke critically of Bankei's laid-back approach, and also of other sects and schools where practice fell short of his own unremitting standards. For him, the quest for Enlightenment was an heroic life-and-death venture to which one should commit everything. There was, however, a less severe, aesthetic side to his nature that expressed itself through the Zen arts of calligraphy, painting and poetry. He was also concerned with propagating Buddhism among ordinary people, and in this context he was prepared to relax a little and make a few concessions to human frailty.

Hakuin is now generally regarded as the revitalizer and reformer of the Rinzai system of training, and his influence, unlike that of Bankei, has been a lasting one. In particular, he revised and extended the koan system, organizing it into a strict programme of formal study. To 'pass' one koan is not enough. After every 'breakthrough' one must forge ahead to new thresholds. Three requirements are necessary in order to be able to meet the challenge – great faith, great doubt and great perseverance. Great doubt, or 'raising the great ball of doubt', an extreme state of spiritual intensity, is particularly emphasized. It is like 'a pair of wings that advances you along the way':

> *'When a person faces the great doubt, before him there is in all directions only a vast and empty land without birth and without death, like a huge plain of ice extending 10,000 miles ... Within his heart there is not the slightest thought or emotion, only the single word Mu [lit. 'No' or 'Not']. It is just as though he were standing in complete emptiness.'*
> *(The zen master Hakuin: Selected Writings, translated by P B Yampolsky.)*

We have already observed Hakuin's own intense struggles with the koan Mu, but the fact is that the stress of them made him seriously ill. Fortunately he was able to cure himself of this 'Zen sickness' by rerouting the vital energy to the area below the navel (tanden). The precise method is outlined in his texts, *Orategama and Yosenkanna.* This touches upon an alchemical aspect of Zen that goes right back to its roots in China and derives from Taoism. It presumes that spiritual practice collects vital energy and that this energy can be used to break through to Enlightenment.

ABOVE KOREAN ZEN BUDDHISM TENDS TO BE LESS MARTIAL AND LESS FORMAL THAN ITS JAPANESE COUNTERPART.

KOREAN ZEN (SON)

The characteristics of Korean Zen are rather different from those of the Japanese variety. It is both less martial and formal, and a little more earthy. There is also strong emphasis on the Vinaya, and both the bhikshu and bhikshuni orders have survived. Nuns have their own nunneries, and their status is not materially lower than that of the monks. Generally, Son preserves something of the flavour of classic Ch'an, and, in a limited way, has been transmitted to the modern West.

When the Rinzai tradition was first brought into Korea from China, it met with local resistance. This did not stifle it but it did force it to embrace elements of other traditions. A syncretistic Zen consequently emerged in the form of the Chogye order, founded by Chinul (1158–1210). Between the 13th and the mid-20th centuries, Buddhism was eclipsed by Confucianism, but the Chogye order emerged again in 1945, at the end of the long Japanese occupation, on an upsurge of nationalistic feeling.

WESTERN ZEN

For most of this century there has been a two-way traffic of Westerners going to Japan to study Zen and Japanese teachers coming to the West. The result is that both the Japanese Rinzai and Soto traditions have been transmitted here and numerous centres established.

The emphasis in Western centres has mainly been on promoting lay practice, though in some the forms of Japanese monasticism, or quasi-monasticism with married 'monks' and 'nuns', have been established. Everywhere, however, the centre of activity is the zendo or meditation hall, which is usually a model of Japanese-style order and simplicity, with a shrine at the far end and neat rows of zafus or meditation cushions facing each other across an empty central aisle. It is here that regular sittings take place, and periods of intensive retreat known as sesshin. Following tradition, Soto students sit facing the wall and engage in their 'just sitting' practice, while Rinzai students face each other and, if so instructed by their teacher, engage in koan study. From time to time an official may march around the room, carrying a stick known as a keisaku. Those meditators who are becoming drowsy or losing muscle-tone may ask to be struck smartly on the shoulder muscles with this. There is likely to be chanting too, the rhythm beaten out on a mokugyo or 'wooden fish'; also much bowing and impersonal formality. Everything is regulated by strict rules, and this lends the atmosphere an edge of severity and purposefulness.

Because of the traditions of direct transmission and lineage, the Zen master or teacher – who may bear the title roshi ('old master') – continues to be of central importance in Western Zen. Students should have regular interviews with him (or her) and during the course of these a fairly intense relationship may be built up. Ideally a teacher should be able to read how students are progressing, note their blockages and guide or push them forwards. A sizeable amount of power is, of course, invested in this role – its origins go back to feudal models – and unfortunately this has been abused by some less than impeccable teachers, resulting in quite serious crises at a few Western centres.

Korean monastic practice incorporates three main elements: study, meditation (Son) and chanting (a Pure Land element). There are separate halls for each of these activities in the monasteries, and monks or nuns are free to specialize in whichever they find most conducive. Study focuses mainly on the Zen records and Mahayana sutras, chanting on the repetition of the names of the Buddha and the Bodhisattvas, and meditation on sitting and koan or hwadu practice. Usually a monk or nun will work on one hwadu, a koan-like question, throughout their training, most probably the ultimate riddle: 'What is it?'

Monks and nuns come together for two three-month meditation retreats in the winter and summer seasons.

PURE LAND

Shakyamuni Buddha is said to have saved himself 'by his own efforts alone', and this streak of spiritual self-help runs right through Buddhism. You will still hear people today saying that, 'You have to do it for yourself – no-one else can do it for you,' which is correct, but not altogether true. For faith and devotion perennially arise within the human heart, faith signifying belief that an external agency can help the individual spiritually, and devotion a deep gratitude for the source of that help. There have been such elements in Buddhism from the earliest times. To practise within the Buddhist tradition is in fact to display faith in that tradition. To bow before an image of a buddha or bodhisattva, a teacher or a monk or nun is to show both faith and devotion. So is to light incense, to copy or recite the scriptures, to carve images, to endow temples and monasteries, to feed the Sangha and so on. Such tendencies grew as the religion itself developed, particularly during its Mahayana phase.

An important early devotional practice was that of Buddhanusmrti or 'Recollection of the Buddha'. This is done by bringing the Buddha to mind, reciting his name, and by visualizing his image and/or his Pure Land or field of activity, which might be either a physical or a transcendental 'place' depending upon the sophistication of the individual view. It is also possible to go beyond recollection of the Buddha as a physical being to a more formless kind of recollection. The benefits to be derived from such practices are considerable – one might have a vision of the Buddha, or one might attain profound meditative states.

With the rise of the Mahayana we find the emergence of a number of cults of divine buddhas and bodhisattvas, such as Avalalokiteshvara, Maiijushri, Maitreya and Kshitigarbha. Each has his (or her) own Pure Land. Those drawn to these cults will recollect and worship these divinities in various ways, and pray for them to intercede spiritually on their behalf.

CHINESE PURE LAND

Though the devotional strand in Buddhism was just one strand alongside others, a separate tendency did establish itself and a distinct school eventually emerged. This was the Pure Land school, which grew out of the cult of Amitabha, the Buddha of Infinite Light.

Though Pure Land historians produced the obligatory line of patriarchs going right back to the Buddha and including such Indian luminaries as Vasubandhu and Nagarjuna, the school undoubtedly reached its full flowering in China. It is based on the legend, recorded in the *Larger Sukhavati-vyuha Sutra*, of an ultra-bodhisattvic monk named Dharmakara, later to become the buddha Amitayus ('Infinite Life' – an aspect of Amitabha), who vowed to create a Pure Land of peerless splendour and not accept Supreme Enlightenment until all sentient beings so wishing had been reborn there. The pious dead would emerge from lotus buds into this Pure Land, the Western Paradise of Suichavati, where all defilements would be rapidly expunged and Nirvana attained in just one more lifetime.

This legend inspired pious Chinese Pure Landers to be in the best frame of mind at the moment of death in order to proceed smoothly to Sukhavati. Many chose their hour of death in advance, took a bath, lit incense and sat upright to await the end, well secluded from grieving relations who might upset their state of mind. However,

ABOVE AMITABHA, THE BUDDHA OF INFINITE LIGHT. THE PURE LAND SCHOOL GREW OUT OF THE CULT OF AMITABHA.

101

was this Sukhavati a 'real place', a heaven with tangible features and adornments, or a metaphor for Enlightenment itself? The answer to this question would again depend upon the sophistication of the individual view.

Also important to Pure Land is the old Buddhist myth of the 'Last Days of the Dharma', which maintains that, after an initial period of vitality, the Buddha-dharma will enter a declining phase and finally a long dark age will set in when conditions will be so inimical that it will be impossible to achieve anything by one's own spiritual efforts alone. All one can do is throw oneself upon the mercy of a benign buddha like Amitayus-Amitabha, whose compassionate Other Power can achieve what cannot be done by the exercise of Own Power. Sixth century China, with its despotic governments, Buddhist persecutions, degenerate priests and prevailing desolation, seemed a perfect image of this predicted dark age, and the Pure Land cult consequently became very popular.

Three early Chinese patriarchs are of especial importance: T'an-luan (476–542), Tao-ch'o (562–645) and Shan-tao (613–681).

THE FIVE PRACTICES OF CHINESE PURE LAND

T'an-luan delineated five practices:

1 To make prostrations to Amitabha and wish to be reborn
   in his Pure Land.
2 To sing the praises of Amitabha and recite his name (in the
   formula, Namu O-mi-to-fo – 'Prostrations to Amitabha').
3 To vow to be reborn in his Pure Land.
4 To visualize Amitabha and his Pure Land.
5 To transfer merit to other living beings.

He also believed that the name of Amitabha encapsulated all
that this buddha stands for, so, like the dharani or magical phrases
of the early Buddhists, the recitation of Name in the formula
O-mi-to-fo ('Prostrations to Amitabha Buddha', known as the
Nien-fo) possessed spiritual power that could ensure the
practitioner rebirth in the Pure Land.

Tao-ch'o, who argued that the recitation of Amitabha's name is a
particularly suitable practice for the present dark age, transmitted the
Pure Land teachings to Sh'an-tao, who 'systematized Pure Land
thought and brought it to its highest peak of development in China'.
(*Shinran's Gospel of Pure Faith*, Alfred Bloom.)

He is also the author of the parable of the Two Rivers and the
White Path:

A Pure Land Everyman, travelling westwards, finds his way
contracted to a thin white path running between two rivers: one of
water and one of fire. Behind, robbers and wild beasts are baying at
his heels. With almost certain death at all sides, what can he do but
forge ahead? He is encouraged by a man calling from the opposite
bank, who promises that if he does so with 'single-heartedness and

true thought' he will be protected. He walks on and duly reaches the western shore safely.

This allegorically depicts the Pure Land view of man's place in the world. It is a horrendously dangerous predicament. The only hope is to seek salvation in the Western Paradise of Amitabha. The moment a practitioner decides to do this with complete faith, help comes from the 'other side'.

Throughout its history Buddhism has tended to be the preserve of the members of an intellectual, spiritual and social élite, and the focus has almost everywhere been in the monasteries. Pure Land Buddhism, however, has more general appeal. It offers an 'easy practice' that can be implemented in the world, without becoming a monk or nun; and it promises salvation to everyone through Amitabha's vows – to those still entrammelled in the passions, even to those who have committed serious crimes. Profound study and meditation are moreover distrusted as they are seen as leading to intellectual and spiritual arrogance.

Pure Land was therefore the first really democratic form of Buddhism, stressing humility rather than attainment, and as such became hugely successful among ordinary Chinese. Pious societies were spawned under its auspices, such as the White Lotus Society, which developed into a sizeable property-owning movement before eventually being suppressed. In its heyday, the good works of its devotees included providing public amenities (bath-houses, hostels, mills, etc.), donating cloth, copying sutras and hosting vegetarian banquets. It was unusual in having married clergy and allowing women to play a prominent part in its affairs. Of the various schools that burgeoned in T'ang dynasty China, only Pure Land and Ch'an (Zen) had the vitality to survive the great persecution of 845.

Very little Chinese Pure Land tradition has been transmitted to Europe, but it is well represented in North America. It was first introduced there in the late-19th century by the thousands of Chinese immigrants coming to work in the California Gold Rush and on the Union Pacific Railroad.

JAPANESE PURE LAND

Once transmitted to Japan, Pure Land became concentrated and simplified: the remaining vestiges of Self Power, including residues of 'hard practice', were stripped away, and primary importance placed upon the Nembutsu (the recitation of the name of Amitabha, known in Japan as Amida, in the formula Namu Amida Butsu), and ultimately on pure faith and grace. Again, its propagation was helped by the fact that the grim Pure Land world-view of Mappo resonated with the social realities of Japanese life at the end of the Heian Era and the beginning of the Kamakura. Civil strife, famine, disease, social breakdown and other evils made ordinary people very receptive to the notion that they were living in degenerate times and so were in need of some special method (or non-method) of salvation.

Two figures are of particular importance in Japanese Pure Land: Honen Shonin (1133–1212), founder of the Jodo-shu ('Pure Land School'), and his disciple, Shinran Shonin (1173–1262), founder of the Jodo Shin-shu ('True Pure Land School').

104

As a Tendai monk, Honen was sincere and dedicated, but he gradually became convinced that he lived in a fallen age and despaired of making any spiritual progress, even by pursuing the Amidist practices applied within the Tendai school. Only the 'easy practice' of the Nembutsu possessed any efficacy, he felt. Even one utterance was sufficient to ensure salvation, though continuous recitation was a healthy discipline, keeping the mind centred on the

LEFT THE KINKAKU-JI, THE GOLDEN TEMPLE, KYOTO, JAPAN. ORIGINALLY CONSTRUCTED IN 1397, THE TEMPLE WAS REBUILT IN 1955.

ultimate goal. In 1175 Honen left the Tendai school and began to teach according to his own convictions. A highly respected and effective monk, he attracted large followings, but this provoked the jealousy of other sects, who eventually managed to get his movement suppressed. In 1207 Honen, along with several disciples, was exiled to a distant province. He was allowed to return to the capital in 1211, a year before his death.

Honen is not regarded as an innovator. He did not advance Pure Land teaching any further than Shan-tao; but he did lay the foundation for an independent Pure Land movement in Japan. Shinran too served an early spiritual apprenticeship as a Tendai monk, and his efforts again merely led to frustration and conflict. He came to feel that he was an utterly hopeless case: ridden with lust and ego, vain, greedy, sinful ... Tainted in fact by all the vices, he was incapable even of performing a simply decent act let alone of saving himself spiritually. Later, he met Honen and the Pure Land teachings and, since he was convinced that he was damned in any case, decided that he had nothing to lose by embracing them. He was banished along with Honen in 1207, and married in exile – he eventually fathered six children - thereby precipitating himself into a limbo of 'neither priest nor layman'. Afterwards, fully adopting the Mahayana view that Samsara is Nirvana, he rejected the dichotomy of lay life and monastic life, and propounded the view that the passions, far from needing to be expunged, are necessary to salvation. In 1211, he was pardoned along with Honen and later went with his family to preach in the Kanto area, where he attracted a considerable following. He receded into rather active retirement in Kyoto in 1235, continuing to teach, study and write. In 1262, lying on his right hand side, 'his head toward the north and his face to the west', he died with the name of the Amida on his lips.

Shinran probed deeper than Honen and came to the conclusion that the actual recitation of the Nembutsu is not as important as the underlying quality of faith, which he equated with the Buddha-nature itself. Faith cannot, however, be contrived by an effort of will

– an effort of Self Power. It is pure grace: a gift bestowed by Amida, whom Shinran regarded as the ultimate Buddha and, in his formless aspect, one with the pure Dharmakaya. The Nembutsu itself bubbles forth as a natural expression of gratitude once faith is given. Concomitant with faith is a sense of the utter futility of Own Power, but this does not lead to self-rejection. On the contrary, it allows one to accept oneself totally, vices and all – one is saved in spite of them.

There is a tendency in the West for Pure Land Buddhism to be down-graded as a low-level spiritual path: a kind of Buddho-Christianity for simple souls incapable of shaping up to the demands of, say, Zen or Tantric practice. This is, however, a misrepresentation. Stripping away the theology and mythology, what Pure Land is saying is that we must let go of all self-initiated activity, have complete faith in the Buddha-nature within and allow it to function in its own mysterious way without interference from the thinking mind. In this way it is not very different from Zen – or other forms of Buddhism. The Nembutsu concentrates and clears the mind, and focuses on the Buddha-nature within.

The Pure Land schools of Honen and Shinran survive to this day, and have been highly successful at the popular level in Japan. They still eschew monasticism and all the frills and excrescences of religious life, concentrating on a simple theology of faith and Nembutsu practice that can be applied in everyday life. Japanese Pure Land Buddhism has also been transmitted to Europe and North America, but has not been particularly successful.

NICHIREN

There is much talk nowadays of Buddhism as 'the fastest growing religion in the West'. Ironically, the brand of Buddhism attracting the largest number of new followers is regarded by many as the least representatively Buddhist of all the schools. This is the Nichiren Sho-shu or 'True Nichiren School', the most successful of the various sub-schools that trace their roots back to Kamakura Era Japan and a Tendai monk named Nichiren Shonin (1222–1282). Today, Nichiren Sho-shu propagates an attractive form of 'Designer Buddhism' with an uncomplicated central chanting practice that draws pop and soap opera stars, fashion and media operators – and hordes of mainly young people.

Nichiren himself was a product of the same fraught milieu as Honen and Shinran. Like them, Nichiren became convinced that he was living in the degenerate age of Mappo, but, having been ordained into the Tendai school, he became convinced that the *Lotus Sutra* embodies the true teachings of Shakyamuni Buddha and that complete faith in it is the sole key to salvation. Other Buddhist schools, he came to believe, did not merely disseminate futile teachings and practices; they were downright pernicious insofar as they diverted people from the One True Path. Not that one had to deeply study and reflect upon the *Lotus Sutra*, however. The text's title encapsulated the totality of truth in the universe and as such was an embodiment of Shakyamuni Buddha. As a practice, therefore, Nichiren prescribed the Daimoku or chanting of the formula Namu-myoho-renge-kyo – 'Homage to the Lotus Sutra of the True Law'.

Nichiren started to proselytise in 1253 – and from the start there was a strong political dimension to his work. He not only unrelentingly denounced the other schools – he regarded this as a religious practice in itself – but called upon the authorities to suppress them. All the natural and social calamities of the time stemmed from failure to embrace the *Lotus Sutra* and toleration of heterodox schools, he declared. And in 1268, when a Mongol invasion threatened, he warned that only faith in the *Lotus* could save Japan. Such aggressive outspokenness naturally alienated the other schools, who in their turn called upon the authorities to suppress Nichiren. He was physically attacked several times and exiled twice. An attempt was also made to execute him, but this miscarried and merely served to vindicate his own sense of righteousness. In fact, all efforts to suppress him merely fired up his own sense of divine mission. Nichiren was eventually pardoned. He lived for a time in a secluded mountain retreat, and died at Ikegami.

Schisms arose within the Nichiren school after the founder's death, one cause of controversy being relations with other schools. Some groupings favoured a more moderate approach, while others advocated the hard line of 'neither to receive nor to give'. Nichiren Sho-shu is definitely of the latter, tracing its spiritual roots back to a 13th century hard-liner named Nikko, although actually founded in 1937 by a pragmatic educator named Tsunesaburo Makiguchi (1871–1944). As a movement with the alternative title of Soka Gakkai ('Value Creating Society') it burgeoned along with other 'new religions' after the military defeat of 1945, when the Japanese suffered a grave collective trauma. Its first leader during the post-War period was Josei Toda (1900–1958), who promoted it so successfully, if controversially), that by 1960 it could claim the loyalty of 750,000 households. Toda was succeeded by Daisaku Ikeda (b.1928), who, judging from the movement's newsletters, spends much time discussing peace with world political leaders. Ikeda founded a political party, the Komeito ('Clean Government Party'), though this has since had to sever its connections with Soka Gakkai.

Nichiren Sho-shu teaches that our destiny lies in our own hands. We must take responsibility for our own lives and make the necessary positive moves to settle our problems and realize our full potential. To these ends, members are actively counselled, helped and supported by the movement, and are encouraged to take up a three-fold practice involving faith, study and chanting. Faith is faith in the power of the Gohoazon, a scroll on which Namu-myoho-renge-kyo is written in mandalic form. The original, penned by Nichiren himself, is lodged in the head temple of Taiseki-ji at the foot of Mount Fuji, but members obtain their own copy and perform Gongyo before it twice daily. Gongyo involves chanting Namu-myoho-renge-kyo, plus selected passages from the *Lotus Sutra*. Finally, there is study of the Buddhist teachings as reformulated by Nichiren and his successors.

All this can be carried out without renouncing the world. Indeed, worldly success is valued within Nichiren Sho-shu, though it is also taught that it cannot lead to lasting happiness. That is only possible by sublimating the lower energies to higher purposes.

Currently, Nichiren Sho-shu is unique in avoiding relations with other Buddhist groups. It still affirms that Nichiren's teachings, which it describes as 'revolutionary' and hence difficult for many other Buddhists to accept, are uniquely suitable for our time. Furthermore, Nichiren himself was, as we have seen, never loath to stir up controversy and hot emotions. He thought them creative forces. Following the founder, therefore, Nichiren Sho-shu maintains the old tradition of shakubuku or vigorous (some might say aggressive) proselytizing.

Other Nichiren sub-schools that have been brought to the West, albeit less successfully than Nichiren Sho-shu, include Reiyukai and its off-shoot Rissho Koseikai; also the Nipponzan Myohoji order founded by Nichidatsu Fujii (1885–1985), a man deeply influenced by Mahatma Gandhi. His white-robed monks and nuns have built peace pagodas in many parts of the world, and work tirelessly and harmoniously with other groups to promote world peace.

THE WESTERN BUDDHIST SPIRITUAL QUEST

CHAPTER EIGHT

The spiritual search to find out who we really are is the greatest adventure. It is the quest for the Holy Grail, for the pearl of great price, for the crock of gold at the end of the rainbow. True, ordinary lives are full of all kinds of seeking and striving. Yet the lesser goals that we set up – wealth, power, love, fame and so on – are really false goals: diversions from what should rightly be our main purpose. At heart we know this, yet time and again we shy away from the challenge, daunted by what it demands of us and what we fear we may have to give up. All the frenzied business of our frantic world, therefore, is really so much running away from our true purpose.

It is an irony that, on the one hand, human ingenuity has probed the depths of space, and, on the other, the minutiae of the atomic world, yet we know least about that to which we live closest – ourselves. Of course there have been people throughout history who have explored this area, and they have left us with many guide-books and maps. We can follow them, but not exactly, for life is an ever-changing labyrinth and we have to find our own routes to its centre.

We usually have to be driven out of our complacency to embark on the spiritual quest. A devastating crisis, much suffering or a growing tiredness of going round and round, repeating the same increasingly meaningless patterns – these are the common precipitating factors. It was certainly so in my own case, when I left a comfortable conventional life in England and set out for India in 1971. Then one had to go to the East if one wanted to find wisdom and teaching. Today it is quite different. There is probably a Buddhist group in your own town, and a centre within a morning's car drive. For during the last 20 years there has been a kind of explosion of Buddhist developments here in the West. Temples, monasteries and centres have sprung up like mushrooms, with the result that one can now probably find better and more accessible teaching in the West than in the East.

The main problem that besets the modern newcomer, therefore, is not difficulty in obtaining teachings but the embarrassment of too much choice. Really, though, we are in a very fortunate position. Because all of the major Buddhist schools and traditions have now been transmitted to the West, we have a clearer view of what is on offer than our former Asiatic co-religionists. We can therefore allow ourselves a period of shopping around, experimenting with this and that in order to find out what suits us best. At some point one usually has to make a commitment to a particular course of study and practice, but it is best not to hurry the process. Commitment will generally arise quite naturally of its own accord when a situation feels right, whereas forcing the issue can lead to trouble. Many teachers and groups are moreover eager to recruit and will sometimes subtly (and sometimes not so subtly!) pressure a newcomer to join their party. On the other hand, many newcomers eagerly desire the consolations of belonging and so often make their choices for the wrong reasons.

Once committed, guard against running away. When Buddhism really begins to 'work', things often get difficult – sometimes very difficult. One may, for instance, have to face things in oneself that one has been dodging for years. The ego does not open itself to new growth without a struggle either – and sometimes an intense one, for every advance demands a kind of death to one's old self. And there are phases when things seem to go dead, like walking through endless, monotonous mud and sleet; or when agonizing doubts or fears arise.

On the other hand, do not feel afraid to leave a group or teacher when it is clear that they have ceased to work for you. Again there can be gross or subtle pressure against going: it may be stigmatized as defection, disloyalty or failure. But remember, Shakyamuni Buddha himself was not afraid to leave his teachers when he had absorbed all they had to teach him. Nor was he deterred from discarding practices he had decided were not useful from fear that fellow practitioners would spurn or deride him. Always, however, be watchful: delve into your own motivations, check your responses and feelings and keep a clear eye on what is happening around you, avoiding the extremes of being a destructive critic or a starry-eyed naive. The Buddhist Way is the middle way – and it is all about learning. If you do decide to leave a group or teacher, do so if possible in the proper way, with appropriate gratitude.

Always be realistic and do not fall prey to illusions, especially collective ones. One illusion that besets many newcomers is that religion is good per se, so they expect all the people and institutions they encounter to be thoroughly benign. In fact, with rare exceptions, religious people and institutions are much like worldly ones. They have their dark as well as their light sides. So be watchful on this account, and then perhaps you will not be too disillusioned if, for instance, your teacher, though possessing undeniable virtues and talents, also turns out to have feet of clay.

Also do not be bedazzled by charismatic teachers, or ones with mass followings, or great fame, power or worldly wealth. True teachers have perennially kept a low profile, living in seclusion, not seeking crowds or worldly success. What they taught was difficult, for the few rather than for the many. Those who successfully mass-market spiritual teachings often do so by watering them down and adding seductive sweeteners.

Be careful too of teachers and groups that pressure you for money or services. The Dharma is said to be beyond price, something that should be freely given. A monk does not ask for dana; he waits for it silently. It should be left up to you to contribute as and when and to what extent you feel fit. Try for your part to be generous, however, not least because generosity fosters spiritual growth.

We go to teachers and groups at the beginning because we need information, guidance and the support of like-minded people. But always the main aim in Buddhism is to help the individual to become free, autonomous, self-reliant. The teacher or group that helps you achieve this is therefore healthy and right-directed. Sadly today, however, there exist many cults that do not liberate their devotees but in effect stunt their development and deprive them of their autonomy. This happens because it is possible for a guru to go astray, and also because the devotee can collude in his or her own exploitation and enslavement. As it is hard to grow up and become an adult, there is always the temptation to look for the ultimate good parent, someone who will make one's decisions and mould one's life.

Always, therefore, maintain a centre of strength and self-reliance within yourself. Do not be pressured out of it. Remember that, as an adult, whatever you think, say or do is your own responsibility. It cannot be handed over to another. And resist the temptation to get too close to a teacher so as to enjoy his or her approval, or to become special, like a favoured son or daughter. Do not stand too far off either. There is a Tibetan saying that the guru is like a fire. Stand too close and you will get burned; stand too far away and you will not get the benefit of any heat – in fact you will freeze!

If the spiritual quest is a great adventure, it must have its difficulties and dangers. Nothing worthwhile is ever achieved by staying at home in safety and comfort. One has to throw oneself into the unknown and brave its mysteries. There are many pitfalls on the path, some of which we have touched upon above, but the greatest of all is spiritual inflation. This is a dire condition in which the ego is enlarged, blown up like a balloon. In traditional terms, it means that we are not dealing with a human being but one engulfed by primordial energies – a demonaic being in fact. This can happen because tremendous psycho-spiritual energies are generated by practice, especially in Tantra. These energies are not simply good in themselves; they are neutral and can be turned to any number of purposes. They can certainly be used to allow us to grow beyond ourselves, to transcend the ego; but the ego can also appropriate them and use them for its own selfish ends. Gurus and teachers are particularly vulnerable to this, for they enjoy power, prestige and public acclaim and so are very susceptible to corruption. It is difficult not to have your head turned when dozens of people stare at you in wide-eyed awe every day. You easily begin to think you are special – unless you maintain close awareness and keep the tendency in check. Inflation makes authentic spiritual development impossible, because an inflated ego is so much more difficult to let go of than an ordinary one.

How to detect inflation? Watch out for the presence of the power complex: the desire to rule and control. This often goes with a certain ruthlessness and contempt for the well-being of others, as though they are of no account and so can be used and abused at will, whereas the guru is great and nothing should be allowed to stand in the way of his or her manifest destiny. An intense dislike of being disagreed with, questioned or criticized are other symptoms; also an eagerness to spend time with and recruit the rich and famous. A liking for titles and fine robes, too, hearing the sound of one's own voice proclaiming inspired truth, and little personal indulgences and concessions, including sometimes a laxness in practice, as though, having 'got there', it is no longer necessary to keep up basic disciplines.

Every practitioner, even the beginner, should be vigilant at all times. This is the basic safeguard, and must be kept up particularly at times when things seem to be going well and one thinks one is 'making progress'. In any case, never regard 'spiritual achievements' as personal gains.

Also do not use Buddhism as an escape from the world or the problems of social living. It is easy to get hooked on a kind of 'Ivory Tower Buddhism', where the rest of the world can go hang while you concentrate on the great task of your own spiritual salvation. The Buddha himself, when occasion demanded, was never reluctant to intervene in social situations; and he even made political pronouncements. On the other hand, one is never so vulnerable to being bushwhacked by the ego as when one is caught up in righteous indignation over a worthy cause. We easily forget then that darkness exists in us too, not just in the evil men whom we oppose. Do we really want to help the world's victims – or bask in the indulgent pleasure of being 'one of the goodies'?

Do not expect too much of yourself at the beginning. Practise regularly and conscientiously, but do not become some kind of spiritual athlete trying to break records. You do not have to sit in meditation longer than anyone else, bear more pain in your knees, read more books. As a matter of fact, that driven, competitive energy will probably wear you out pretty quickly.

115

In the same way, do not turn your practice into a kind of penance, flagellating yourself with it. We Westerners do not really think very well of ourselves; we suffer from deep-seated guilts and self-hatred. Because of this, we are hard on ourselves – and hard on others too. Look what brutality has been inflicted on the world in

RIGHT BE PATIENT IN YOUR MEDITATION PRACTICE. REAL AND LASTING CHANGE IS A LONG, SLOW BUSINESS.

the name of righteous religion. What we really need, therefore, is to soften up, to open our hearts and allow our innate but stifled warmth to emerge. This is indeed what Buddhist practice is very much about, especially the Mahayana variety with its primary emphasis on compassion.

There are forms of Buddhist practice, however, that are very hard and harsh. While those may have been appropriate in the areas and situations in which they were originally developed, it is doubtful whether they are always beneficial for Westerners, who often need more of the opposite treatment. Some people are drawn to those hard forms, though. Perhaps they feel that, through them, they can place themselves beyond suffering. But you do not conquer suffering by becoming like a block of ice or a rigid, programmed automaton. In Buddhism, we train ourselves to be open and fully vulnerable to the sting of suffering – but able to take it and survive. We train ourselves to be real human beings.

While being aware of the pitfalls of the path, do not be deterred by them. You will certainly make mistakes. We all make mistakes – and they are all right if we learn from them. You may have your ideals smashed; people in whom you invest great trust may let you down; but do not cling to the negativity such experiences inevitably produce. Let go of it, absorb the lesson – and walk on.

Always try to remain open. You cannot learn if you are not open-minded. You never know from which unlikely direction your next important teaching is going to come. Unfortunately, though, probably because they have been hurt or disillusioned early on, many Westerners close up and so cannot take in anything that might change or even help them. Openness means being fully alert and aware, not blocking anything out, not avoiding things (especially unpleasant things), not saying No, not refusing to meet the world on anything but one's own terms. It means letting go of the need to control. However, be realistic too; do not continue to be open when it is clear it is no longer sensible to be so. Openness is not synonymous with naïveté or gullibility. The middle way again.

It is all, however, as I said at the start, a great adventure – and especially for beginners, who are often so much more fresh and open than longterm seekers. The Zen master Shunryu Suzuki Roshi, who worked for many years in the US, had good reason to call his most famous book *Zen Mind, Beginner's Mind.* I remember with great nostalgia the early days of my own quest, as I ranged for many months through India as the spirit moved me. I had expected to meet great gurus, but the swamis and sadhus who confidently proclaimed their saintly accomplishments in the various ashrams and holy places I visited failed to impress me. I was not let down, though; I received my teaching from India herself, that deeply spiritual land where, whether one goes with it or resists, one is precipitated into stark confrontation with this amazing business of life in which we find ourselves so mysteriously caught up. Wonderful experiences and insights came, not earned but free gifts bestowed by the Unknowable with bountiful generosity.

Do not be intimidated. Have confidence in your own spiritual potentiality, your ability to find your own unique way. Learn from others certainly, and use what you find useful, but also learn to trust your own inner wisdom. Have courage. Be awake and aware. Remember too that Buddhism is not about being 'a Buddhist'; that is, obtaining a new identity tag. Nor is it about collecting head-knowledge, practices and techniques. It is ultimately about letting go of all forms and concepts and becoming free. So be prepared to cut through all superfluous accretions and go for the gold of the spiritual core. It is certainly there, within – and, so the greatest masters assure us, it is not as difficult to get at as we often tend to think.

117

GLOSSARY

Abhisheka The rite of initiation.

Anatman Buddhist teaching that originated as a reaction against the brahmanical concept of atman.

Anitya Impermanence.

Arhat The 'noble one', one who is assured of Enlightenment.

Atman The soul or self, which according to Brahman teachings is one in reality with Brahman – the ultimate reality.

Avidya Delusion, ignorance.

Bardo In Tibetan Buddhism, the intermediate state that intervenes between one life and another.

Bhumi A stage on the Bodhisattva Path.

Buddhavacana The word of Buddha.

Bodhicitta Enlightened mind.

Bodhisattva One who is motivated by compassionate zeal to help others on the path to their own Enlightenment.

Dharma The path of liberation, the truth, the way.

Dharmas The ultimate building blocks of reality.

Dhyana Bliss state, state of trance.

Duhkha Suffering.

Dvesha Anger, hatred.

Karma The consequences of one's actions of body, speech and mind.

Karuna Compassion.

Mandala Symbolic models of the cosmos.

Mantra Sacred formulae.

Nirvana The escape from Samsara (cyclic existence).

Paramita Perfected virtue.

Parinirvana 'Beyond Nirvana'. The State that one who has reached Nirvana passed into after death.

Prajña Wisdom.

Prajñaparamita Perfection of Wisdom.

Pratimoskha Code of rules for monks and nuns.

Samadhi A state of complete concentration and absorbed contemplation.

Samsara The cycle of death and rebirth.

Sangha A community of Buddhist monks.

Shunyata Emptiness.

Siddhas Adepts.

Skandhas The five basic components that make up the individual person.

Sukha Pleasant feeling.

Tantra Mystical and magical Buddhist writings.

Tantrika A person who is an adept of Tantra.

Trishna Thirst, craving, desire.

Upaya Skilful means for arriving at direct perception of truth.

Vajra A Buddhist symbol derived from the mythical thunderbolt of the Indian god Indra.

Vipaka The fruit that comes from a preceding cause or action.

Further Reading

THERAVADA TEXTS

The Pali Text Society (73 Lime Walk, Headington, Oxford OX3 7AD, UK) has made the *Pali Canon* available in English translation. Its publications include volumes of suttas of the *Digha Nikaya* (*Long Discourses*), *Majjhima Nikaya* (*Middle Length Discourses*) and *Samyutta Nikaya* (*Kindred Sayings*).

MAHAYANA TEXTS

A Guide to the Bodhisattva's Way of Life, Shantideva, trans.
S Batchelor, Library of Tibetan Works & Archives, Dharamsala, 1979
The Short Prajitaparamita Texts, trans. E Conze, Luzac,
London, 1973
Buddhist Wisdom Books, trans. E Conze, George Allen & Unwin,
London, 1958
The Awakening of Faith in the Mahayana, Ashvaghosa, trans.
Y S Hakeda, Columbia University Press, New York, 1967
The Holy Teaching of Vimalakirti, trans. R H F Thurman,
Pennsylvania State University Press, University Park, 1986
The Lankavatara Sutra, trans. D T Suzuki, Routledge, London, 1932
Seven Works of Vasubandhu, trans. S Anaker, Motilal Banarsidass,
Delhi, 1984
The Threefold Lotus Sutra, trans. Kato, Tamura et al, Kosei
Publishing Co, Tokyo, 1987
The Avatamsaka Sutra, (3 vols.) trans. T Cleary, Shambhala,
Boston, 1985-7

ZEN TEXTS

The Zen Teaching of Huang-po, trans. J Blofeld, The Buddhist
Society, London, 1968
The Record of Rinzai, trans. I Schloegl, The Buddhist Society,
London, 1975

The Platform Sutra of the 6th Patriarch (Hui Neng), trans.
P Yampolsky, Columbia University Press, New York, 1967
Zen Master Hakuin: Selected Writings, trans. P Yampolsky,
Columbia University Press, New York, 1971
The Blue Cliff Record (3 vols.) trans. T & J C Cleary, Shambhala,
Boulder 1977
Swampland Flowers: The Letters & Lectures of Zen Master Ta Hui,
trans. C Cleary, Grove Press, New York, 1977
Bankei Zen, trans. P Haskel, Grove Press, New York, 1984
The Zen Teaching of Instantaneous Awakening, Hui Hai, trans.
J Blofeld, Buddhist Publishing Group, Leicester, 1987 reprint
Shobogenzo: Zen Essays by Dogen Zenji, trans. T Cleary, University
of Hawaii Press, Honolulu, 1986
Two Zen Classics: Mumonkan & Hekiganroku, trans. K Sekida,
Weatherhill, New York & Tokyo, 1977

TANTRIC TEXTS

The Kalachakra Tantra: Rite of Initiation, trans. J Hopkins, Wisdom
Publications, London, 1985
Tantra in Tibet: The Great Exposition of Secret Mantra, Tsongkhapa,
George Allen & Unwin, London, 1976

GENERAL

The World of Buddhism, eds. Béchert and Gombrich, Thames &
Hudson, London, 1985
The Buddhist Handbook, John Snelling, Century-Hutchinson,
London, 1987

REFERENCE

A Popular Dictionary of Buddhism, Christmas Humphreys, Arco,
London, 1962
Buddhist Dictionary, Nyanatiloka Thera, Buddhist Publication
Society, Kandy, 1980
The Buddhist Directory, The Buddhist Society, London, 1987

Zen Buddhism in North America, A History & Directory, Zen Lotus Society, Toronto, 1986

THE BUDDHIST WORLD-VIEW
Buddhist Cosmology, R Kloetzli, Motilal Banarsidass, Delhi, 1983

THE BUDDHA
The Life of the Buddha, Bhikkhu Nyanamoli, Buddhist Publication Society, Kandy, 1971
The Buddha, Trevor Ling, Penguin Books, Harmondsworth, 1973

MEDITATION
Living Buddhist Masters, Jack Komfield, Shambhala Publications, Boulder, 1983 reprint
The Heart of Buddhist Meditation, Nyanaponika Thera, Rider Books, London, 1962
Mahayana Buddhist Meditation: Theory and Practice, ed. Minoru Kyota, University of Hawaii Press, Honolulu, 1978

INDIAN BUDDHISM
History of Indian Buddhism, E Lamotte, trans. S Webb-Boin, Peeters Press, Louvain, 1988
Indian Buddhism, K Warder, Motilal Banarsidass, Delhi, 1970, 1980 reprint

THERAVADA BUDDHISM
What the Buddha Taught, W Rahula, Gordon Frazer, Bedford, 1972.
Cittaviveka, Ajahn Sumedho, Chithurst Forest Monastery, Petersfield, 1983
Theravada Buddhism, R Gombrich, Routledge & Kegan Paul, London, 1988

MAHAYANA BUDDHISM (GENERAL)
Mahayana Buddhism, Paul Williams, Kegan Paul, London, 1989

BUDDHIST PHILOSOPHY

Essentials of Buddhist Philosophy, J Takakusu, Motilal Banarsidass, Delhi, 1975 reprint

The Central Conception of Buddhism (and the Meaning of the World 'Dharma'), T Stcherbatsky, London 1923, Motilal Banarsidass, Delhi, 1970 reprint

The Central Philosophy of Buddhism, T R V Murti, George Allen & Unwin, London, 1955 (A study of the Madhyamaka system.)

Entry into the Inconceivable: An Introduction to Hua-yen Buddhism, Thomas Cleary, University of Hawaii Press, Honolulu, 1983

Hua-yen Buddhism: The Jewel Net of Indra, Francis Cook, Pennsylvania State University Press, University Park, 1981

Studies in the Lankavatara Sutra, D T Suzuki, Routledge, London, 1930

CHINESE BUDDHISM

Buddhism in Chinese History, A F Wright, Stamford University Press, Stamford, 196.

Buddhism in China, K Chen, Princeton University Press, Princeton, 1964

PURE LAND

Shinran's Gospel of Pure Grace, Alfred Bloom, University of Arizona Press, Tucson, Arizona, 1965, 1981 reprint

Plain Words on the Pure Land Way, trans. D Hirota, Ryukoku University, Kyoto, 1989

NICHIREN

Nichiren Shoshu Buddhism, R Causton, Century, London, 1988

CHINESE & JAPANESE ZEN

A History of Zen Buddhism, H Dumoulin, Faber, London, 1968

A First Zen Reader, T Leggett, Charles Tuttle, Tokyo & Rutland, Vermont, 1960

Zen and the Ways, T Leggett, RKP, London, 1978
Taking the Path of Zen, Robert Aitken, Nortji Point Press, San Francisco, 1982
Unsui: A Diary of a Zen Monk, Giei Sato & Eshin Nishimura, University of Hawaii Press, Honolulu, 1973
Empty Cloud: The Autobiography of Chinese Zen Master Xu Yun, trans. C Luk, Element Books, Dorset, 1988

KOREAN ZEN
The Way of Korean Zen, Kusan Sunim, trans. M Fages, Weatherhill, New York & Tokyo, 1985

TIBETAN BUDDHISM
The Jewel in the Lotus, ed. S Batchelor, Wisdom Publications, London, 1987
Advice from a Spiritual Friend, Geshe Rabten & Geshe Dhargyey, Wisdom Publications, London, 1978
The Religions of Tibet, G. Tucci, RKP, London, 1980
Hidden Teachings of Tibet, Tulku Thondup Rinpoche, Wisdom Publications, London, 1986
The Crystal and the Way of Light, Namkhai Norbu Rinpoche, RKP, London, 1986

WESTERN BUDDHISM
Buddhism in Britain, P Oliver, Rider Books, London, 1979
How the Swans Came to the Lake, R Fields, Shambhala, Boston, 1986 (Buddhism in the USA) revised edition

BUDDHISM AND WESTERN PSYCHOLOGY
Psychotherapy East and West, Alan Watts, Ballantine Books, New York, 1961
Buddhism and Western Psychology, Nathan Katz, Shambhala, Boulder, 1983
Psychology and the East, C G Jung, RKP, London, 1978

124

INDEX

LOOK AT LIFE...
with a NEW PERSPECTIVE

A series of comprehensive introductions
to key mind, body, spirit subjects

★ **STYLISH AND ACCESSIBLE** ★

★ **STRAIGHTFORWARD AND PRACTICAL** ★

★ **CONTEMPORARY TWO COLOUR DESIGN WITH ILLUSTRATIONS** ★

BOOKS AVAILABLE IN THE SERIES:

1 86204 629 8

1 86204 630 1

1 86204 667 0

1 86204 628 X

1 86204 664 6

1 86204 663 8

1 86204 626 3

1 86204 627 1

1 86204 668 9

1 86204 625 5

1 86204 665 4

1 86204 673 5

ALSO AVAILABLE IN THIS SERIES: ASTROLOGY 1 86204 666 2, BUDDHISM 1 86204 764 2, CHAKRAS 1 86204 765
COLOUR THERAPY 1 86204 766 9, CRYSTAL THERAPY 1 86204 739 1, HERBAL REMEDIES 1 86204 767 7,
I CHING 1 86204 763 4, NUTRITIONAL THERAPY 1 86204 740 5, RUNES 1 86204 762 6,
SHAMANISM 1 86204 761 8, TAI CHI 1 86204 760 X, YOGA 1 86204 759 6